The DC Sniper Shootings

Other titles in Lucent's Crime Scene Investigations series include:

The DC Sniper Shootings

by Craig E. Blohm

LUCENT BOOKS

An imprint of Thomson Gale, a part of The Thomson Corporation

THOMSON
GALE

Detroit • New York • San Francisco • San Diego • New Haven, Conn. • Waterville, Maine • London • Munich

THOMSON

GALE

For Ethan

For more information, contact:
Lucent Books
27500 Drake Rd.
Farmington Hills, MI 48331-3535
Or you can visit our Internet site at http://www.gale.com

LIBRARY OF CONGRESS CATALOGING-IN-PUBLICATION DATA

Blohm, Craig E., 1948–
  The D.C. sniper shootings / by Craig E. Blohm.
    p. cm. — (Crime scene investigations)
  Includes bibliographical references and index.
  ISBN 1-59018-926-4 (hard cover : alk. paper) 1. Serial murder investigation—Washington Suburban Area—Juvenile literature. 2. Serial murders—Washington Suburban Area—Juvenile literature. 3. Criminal snipers—Washington Suburban Area—Juvenile literature. I. Title. II. Title: DC sniper shootings. III. Series: Crime scene investigations series.
  HV8079.H6 B56 2006
  364.152'309753—dc22
                                            2006012237

Printed in the United States of America

Contents

Foreword

The popularity of crime scene and investigative crime shows on television has come as a surprise to many who work in the field. The main surprise is the concept that crime scene analysts are the true crime solvers, when in truth, it takes dozens of people, doing many different jobs, to solve a crime. Often, the crime scene analyst's contribution is a small one. One Minnesota forensic scientist says that the public "has gotten the wrong idea. Because I work in a lab similar to the ones on *CSI*, people seem to think I'm solving crimes left and right— just me and my microscope. They don't believe me when I tell them that it's the investigators that are solving crimes, not me."

Crime scene analysts do have an important role to play, however. Science has rapidly added a whole new dimension to gathering and assessing evidence. Modern crime labs can match a hair of a murder suspect to one found on a murder victim, for example, or recover a latent fingerprint from a threatening letter, or use a powerful microscope to match tool marks made during the wiring of an explosive device to a tool in a suspect's possession.

Probably the most exciting of the forensic scientist's tools is DNA analysis. DNA can be found in just one drop of blood, a dribble of saliva on a toothbrush, or even the residue from a fingerprint. Some DNA analysis techniques enable scientists to tell with certainty, for example, whether a drop of blood on a suspect's shirt is that of a murder victim.

While these exciting techniques are now an essential part of many investigations, they cannot solve crimes alone. "DNA doesn't come with a name and address on it," says the Minnesota forensic scientist. "It's great if you have someone in custody to match the sample to, but otherwise, it doesn't help. That's the investigator's job. We can have all the great DNA evidence in the world, and without a suspect, it will just sit on the shelf. We've all seen cases with very little forensic evidence get solved by the resourcefulness of a detective."

While forensic specialists get the most media attention today, the work of detectives still forms the core of most criminal investigations. Their job, in many ways, has changed little over the years. Most cases are still solved through the persistence and determination of a criminal detective whose work may be anything but glamorous. Many cases require routine, even mind-numbing tasks. After the July 2005 bombings in London, for example, police officers sat in front of video players watching thousands of hours of closed-circuit television tape from security cameras throughout the city, and as a result were able to get the first images of the bombers.

The Lucent Books Crime Scene Investigations series explores the variety of ways crimes are solved. Titles cover particular crimes such as murder, specific cases such as the killing of three civil rights workers in Mississippi, or the role specialists such as medical examiners play in solving crimes. Each title in the series demonstrates the ways a crime may be solved, from the various applications of forensic science and technology to the reasoning of investigators. Sidebars examine both the limits and possibilities of the new technologies and present crime statistics, career information, and step-by-step explanations of scientific and legal processes.

The Crime Scene Investigations series strives to be both informative and realistic about how members of law enforcement—criminal investigators, forensic scientists, and others—solve crimes, for it is essential that student researchers understand that crime solving is rarely quick or easy. Many factors—from a detective's dogged pursuit of one tenuous lead to a suspect's careless mistakes to sheer luck to complex calculations computed in the lab—are all part of crime solving today.

Two Bullets

In October 2002, forty-three-year-old Ann Chapman had been working as a cashier for about a year in the Michaels crafts store at the Northgate Plaza Shopping Center in Aspen Hill, Maryland. Wednesday, October 2, had been a routine day for her as she checked out purchases for her customers. Suddenly, at 5:20 P.M. Chapman was startled by a loud crash that rang out over the low hum of noise in the store. "I had just gotten rid of a customer," she later recalled. "I thought a lightbulb blew up."[1] Then she looked up at the illuminated sign over checkout lane number five: It was shaking, and there was a hole in it. This was no lightbulb explosion. In fact, a bullet had smashed through the store's front window, making a dime-size hole in the glass. The bullet then pierced the checkout sign and hit two other cardboard signs, finally lodging itself in the wall of the store about 7 feet (2.1m) from the floor. Chapman was shaken; the bullet had narrowly missed her as she stood at her register.

Two miles (3.2km) away and less than an hour later, James D. Martin stopped at the Shoppers Food Warehouse in Wheaton, Maryland, to pick up some groceries before heading home from work. A program analyst for the National Oceanic and Atmospheric Administration, fifty-five-year-old Martin was active in his church and in the PTA at his son's school. He also helped lead the local Boy Scout troop. A Civil War buff, Martin collected memorabilia from that historic conflict. At 6:02 P.M. Martin had just gotten out of his Mazda pickup truck and was walking toward the supermarket when a boom echoed over the parking lot. At that instant a bullet slammed into Martin's back, severing his spinal cord and cutting the main artery in his body. He immediately pitched forward from the force of the bullet, then collapsed to the ground, motionless. A woman nearby saw him fall and called 911 on her cell phone.

At about the same time, a Montgomery County police officer who was in his cruiser across the street from Shoppers Food Warehouse heard the gunshot. He sped across the busy highway, lights flashing. When he saw Martin lying on the pavement, he knew what had happened and grabbed his radio microphone. "I'm at Shoppers Food Warehouse on Randolph," he shouted. "I've got the sound of a shot. One down."[2] An ambulance soon arrived and emergency medical technicians went to work. They soon gave up, however, for Martin was already dead.

At Montgomery County police headquarters, Detective Patrick McNerney received a call about a homicide in

Investigators search for evidence near a gas station in Fredericksburg, Virginia, where a man was killed by the DC Snipers.

Wheaton. When he arrived at the scene, McNerney set his evidence technicians to work looking for clues to what had happened. Other Montgomery County detectives soon joined McNerney at the supermarket parking lot. They knew they had to find answers to a whole host of questions: Where had the shot come from? Why was Martin targeted, and what was the killer's motive? Had any shoppers in the parking lot seen anything suspicious? And what about the shooting at the Aspen Hill Michaels store? Just two miles (3.2km) and forty-two minutes apart, two bullets had been fired. One was a harmless miss, while the other took the life of an innocent victim. Could they somehow be connected? At this early stage, law enforcement authorities were not sure what it all meant.

By the time it was dark, Martin's body had been removed and his blood washed off the pavement. The detectives planned to return the next day to search again for the forensic evidence they knew would be crucial in identifying the murderer and ultimately putting him or her behind bars. As they prepared to leave the scene, McNerney said the words they all were thinking. "We got a problem," he said. "I think there's a sniper out there."[3]

CHAPTER 1

A Deadly October Day

In October 2002 one of the deadliest sniper sprees in American history began in the suburbs of Washington, DC. The first two shots were fired on Wednesday, October 2. One bullet crashed through the window of a Michaels craft store in Aspen Hill, Maryland, startling employees and customers but injuring no one. The second bullet was fired less than an hour later into the parking lot of a nearby Shoppers Food Warehouse. James D. Martin, a fifty-five-year-old family man, was killed instantly as he walked toward the store from his car. The next day, bewildered law enforcement officers desperately searched for clues as the unknown sniper began taking more innocent lives.

As they did so, James L. "Sonny" Buchanan was performing work of a different sort. Born in Bethesda, Maryland, and raised just a few miles away in Gaithersburg, Buchanan was the youngest child of a former Montgomery County police officer. He was an ambitious young man with a ready smile and a big heart who helped less fortunate kids by mentoring at the local Boys & Girls Club. He also served on the board of the Montgomery County Crime Solvers hotline. After graduating from the University of Maryland with a business degree, he had taken over the family landscaping business, which he ran until he moved to his father's farm in the Virginia mountains. But the thirty-nine-year-old Buchanan regularly returned to Rockville, Maryland, to visit with friends and mow lawns as a favor to former customers.

He was doing just that on the morning of October 3, 2002. Fitzgerald Auto Mall, a longtime customer of Buchanan's landscaping business, is located on busy Rockville Pike just a few miles north of Washington, DC. As morning rush hour traffic on the

James Buchanan was rushed to a hospital in White Flint, Maryland, after being shot in the chest. He was the second of the DC Snipers' victims to die.

pike crawled toward downtown Washington, Buchanan was pushing a green Lawn-Boy mower along the grass behind the auto dealer, adjacent to the parking lot of the nearby White Flint Mall. At 7:41 A.M. a loud bang echoed across the paved lot. Buchanan stopped suddenly and released his grip on the mower. He grabbed his chest and staggered toward the auto mall as the lawn mower continued to chug along by itself. Stumbling and gasping for breath, Buchanan made it about 50 yards (46m) before he collapsed face down on the pavement. Several Fitzgerald employees saw him fall. As one raced to where he lay, parts manager Jim King called 911. "The guy's lawn mower did something, man," King said. "It chopped him

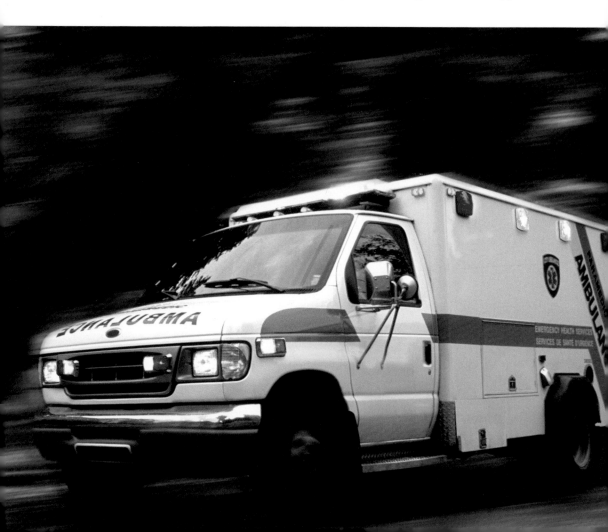

up. He's bleeding real bad."[4] King believed it had to be a lawn mower accident. He could not even imagine that Buchanan had been shot.

Within minutes paramedics arrived on the scene and determined that Buchanan was still alive. He was bleeding profusely from a hole in his chest, but his heart was barely beating. He was rushed to nearby Suburban Hospital and taken directly to the trauma unit, where doctors struggled to save his life. But he had lost too much blood; his heart had stopped and efforts to start it again were unsuccessful.

Still believing Buchanan had died from a freak lawn mower accident, trauma unit doctors took a closer look at his wounds. They discovered a tiny hole in Buchanan's back that could be an entrance wound made by a bullet. A police officer who was at the hospital agreed that the physical evidence did not add up to a simple mowing accident. In fact, Buchanan was the second victim of a sniper's bullet, and the first to die on October 3, 2002. He was not, however, the last.

Innocent Victims

The scene of the sniper's next attack was a Mobil gas station at the busy intersection of Aspen Hill Road and Connecticut Avenue in Aspen Hill. The station was located only three blocks from the Michaels craft store that had been shot at the day before. Shortly after 8:00 A.M. a dark gray taxicab pulled into the station and its driver, Premkumar Walekar, got out. A stout fifty-four-year-old native of Pune, India, Walekar walked to the station's store and bought some gum and a lottery ticket. Then he went back to the gas pumps and began fueling his cab. He was standing by the rear of the cab when a loud shot boomed over the din of rush-hour traffic on Aspen Hill Road. Walekar had a bewildered look on his face as blood began to spread over his clothes. He walked unsteadily toward a van parked at another pump, and when the woman in the van looked up he managed to say, "Call an ambulance,"[5] before collapsing.

The driver of the van, a physician named Caroline Namrow, had just stopped to get gas after dropping her children off at school. She quickly called 911 on her cell phone and then, noticing a passing police car, ran to flag it down. When she returned to the scene she began performing CPR on Walekar until the ambulance arrived a few minutes later and emergency medical technicians (EMTs) took over. As the ambulance sped to Montgomery General Hospital, the EMTs tried to find Walekar's pulse, but it was no use; his heart had stopped. The ambulance crew was advised by radio to stop attempts at resuscitation. It was 8:37 A.M. At that same moment, another call was coming in to the 911 dispatch center. "I need an ambulance and police at Leisure World Plaza," said the frantic caller. "A girl just shot herself."[6]

The woman, Sarah Ramos, was thirty-four years old. A native of El Salvador, she worked as a housekeeper to help make ends meet for her family: a husband and seven-year-old son. On the morning of October 3, Ramos was sitting on a bench outside a Crisp & Juicy chicken restaurant at the Leisure World Plaza in Silver Spring, Maryland. She was reading as she waited to be picked up for her housekeeping job when a loud bang echoed across the plaza. Ramos slumped over; the booklet she had been reading was still in her lap, but now it was soaked with blood. She had not committed suicide, as the startled and confused 911 caller had erroneously thought. Sarah Ramos was the fourth victim of the unknown sniper. She died instantly, the bullet that killed her crashing into a window just behind the bench.

More than an hour passed with no more reports of shootings coming in to the police. Then, at 9:58 A.M., the sniper struck again, this time at a Shell gas station in Kensington, Maryland. Twenty-five-year-old Lori Ann Lewis-Rivera, a nanny and

By the Numbers

3,000
FEET PER SECOND

Velocity of a .223 caliber bullet fired from an assault rifle

the mother of a three-year-old girl, was at the Shell station vacuuming out her minivan. Mechanics working nearby heard a loud noise, and thought there had been a crash on the highway or that an air bag had accidentally deployed. But any notion of an accident was dispelled when they saw Lewis-Rivera lying on the ground next to her van. Within minutes, three bystanders—an intensive care nurse, a county police officer, and a firefighter from the station across the street—struggled to keep Lewis-Rivera alive until an ambulance arrived. For the second time that morning, a shooting victim made the ride to Suburban Hospital. And for the second time, the trauma team desperately tried to save the patient's life. But it was, again, too late. Lewis-Rivera was dead. Trauma surgeon Dr. James Robey noted the similarity with the Sonny Buchanan case he had worked on earlier that morning. "The wound is in the exact same place," Robey remarked. Then he added a chilling comment: "Someone's just picking people off."[7]

Pictured is a bullet hole the DC Snipers put in the window of a Michaels craft store.

The Police Respond

While the sniper was stalking his victims that Thursday morning, Charles Moose, chief of the Montgomery County Police Department, was preparing to attend the funeral of a fellow officer. After the funeral he planned to catch a flight to Minneapolis for a police conference. Forty-nine-year-old Moose had grown up in a predominantly black middle-class neighborhood in Lexington, North Carolina. He had served for nearly ten years as a police officer, first in Portland, Oregon, and then in Montgomery County. Moose was a thoughtful,

Tracking the Invisible

While most clues at a shooting scene are physical objects such as bullet fragments or shell casings, some important evidence can be invisible to the naked eye. Trajectory analysis is the science of using geometry to determine the number and location of the shooter or shooters. A trajectory is the path taken through space by a bullet after it leaves the muzzle of a gun. It takes a minimum of two points to determine the path of a bullet; at a crime scene, these points are usually bullet holes. By measuring the angle between two or more bullet holes, a firearms expert can trace back along an imaginary line made by that angle and determine the point from which the bullet was fired. For example, in the case of the first DC Sniper shooting at the Aspen Hill, Maryland, Michaels store, investigators tracked the path of the bullet through the window and checkout sign to the wall it struck. By analyzing the trajectory, they concluded that the shot was fired from a low position, and that it was probably intended as a kill shot that just missed its mark.

almost shy man who nevertheless had an explosive temper. His personnel file from Portland contained at least four incidents in which his temper got him into trouble, including a run-in with a local department store clerk.

As Moose was beginning to plan his day he received word that a man had been killed while mowing the lawn at the Fitzgerald Auto Mall. At this point, many still thought the lawn mower had somehow caused Buchanan's death. But Moose was not so sure, recalling the murder of James Martin at the Shoppers Food Warehouse the night before. What if this was another shooting? "I remember thinking, *This is strange*," Moose later wrote. "We got murders weeks apart, or even months apart. Two men being shot like that, in less than twenty-four hours, that was strange."[8] But the strangeness was just beginning. A short time later Moose was informed of yet another killing, the slaying of Premkumar Walekar at a Mobil gas station not far from the Michaels store with the bullet-shattered window. This third killing changed Moose's plans for the rest of the day. There would be no attendance at the funeral, no trip to Minneapolis. He donned his bulletproof vest—an item he constantly urged all of his officers to wear—and headed for the latest crime scene.

By the time Moose arrived, the Mobil station had been cordoned off by yellow police tape and several patrol cars were already there. The media, too, began descending on the area, with camera crews unloading equipment from news vans and helicopters hovering noisily overhead. Moose approached detective Terry Ryan of the Major Crimes Division of the Montgomery County Police. "What the hell's going on?" the chief asked. Ryan replied, "You know as much as I do. We're not even sure where he was shot."[9] As more detectives and

Police chief Charles Moose (left) and another officer discuss the sniper case. Moose was in charge of the investigation.

reporters reached the scene, it was obvious to the chief that the rapidly growing case would require coordination. So the Montgomery County mobile command vehicle was called out. A bus that had been converted to include office space, a conference room, and communication equipment, the command vehicle was parked in the lot of a nearby church. By the time the command center was in place, offers of help were already coming in from the Federal Bureau of Investigation (FBI); the Bureau of Alcohol, Tobacco and Firearms; the U.S. Secret Service; and the U.S. Marshals Service. SWAT teams and police helicopters were called out to provide protection and surveillance of the crime scenes.

In his mind, Moose went over what little his officers already knew about the shootings. They were not robberies, because no wallets or purses were taken. They were not the results of domestic quarrels or drug deals gone bad, and they definitely were not suicides. Furthermore, there seemed to be no obvious connection between the victims; they were people of varying races, ages, and income levels. Yet Moose felt there had to be a connection; the shootings were not just a bizarre coincidence. And he wondered about the shooter: Who was he and why was he doing this? "I didn't have any theories," Moose recalls. "I remember thinking the guy could be observing this all, right now, and really enjoying himself."[10]

At the Mobil station Walekar's gray cab still sat at the pumps. Inside the station's office, police were questioning customers and employees to determine whether anyone saw anything that might aid in identifying the killer. But there was little information to go on, no eyewitnesses, and no clues.

Yet because of live TV coverage, the Washington, DC, area now knew that something was going on, and the public would soon want some answers. At 11:19 A.M. Moose held a press conference at the command center, the first of many he would conduct over the next three weeks. "We strongly feel that all these [shootings] are connected," he told reporters. "We don't need panic. . . . I am convinced that someone knows who's doing this. I am convinced that someone has seen something."[11] As it happened, Moose's last statement was correct: Someone had seen something.

The White Truck

That someone was twenty-year-old Juan Carlos Villeda, an immigrant from Guatemala who worked as a landscaper and spoke little English. On the morning of October 3, Villeda was working outside the Leisure World Plaza in Silver Spring when Sarah Ramos was struck and killed by the sniper's bullet. He told John Desoulas, a Spanish-speaking detective, that he had seen a vehicle—a white box truck or perhaps a van—speeding away from the scene of the shooting. According to Villeda, the truck had black or purple writing on it, and it was dented in the rear. He said the truck might have had a ladder rack on it, but he did not remember the license plate number, nor could he give a description of the driver. It was not much to go on, but it was more than Moose and his officers had at the time.

Word of Villeda's observation made its way through the police communications network and eventually onto local news programs. Soon everyone, law enforcement and civilians alike, began looking for a white truck or van that might be linked to the slayings. Complicating the search was the fact that white box truck and cargo vans are ubiquitous in large urban centers such as the Washington, DC, area. Such vehicles are used by numerous businesses as delivery and work vehicles; in fact, a computer search revealed more than seventy thousand of this type of truck in Maryland alone. The Montgomery County Police Department displayed a large picture—a sort of wanted poster—showing what appeared to be a white Chevrolet Astro or Ford Econoline van. Numerous calls to the authorities

Chief of the Investigation

Charles A. Moose was born in August 1953 in New York City, but soon after his birth his family moved to Lexington, North Carolina. Growing up in a solidly middle-class family, Charles seldom got into any real trouble, so he never personally knew a police officer. But he picked up on the local attitude about the police: They were the "bad guys" who beat blacks, trumped up charges, and told nothing but lies.

Charles Moose answers questions about the DC Snipers at a press conference.

By his senior year at the University of North Carolina, Moose was planning to become a lawyer. But a chance meeting with a recruiter from the Portland, Oregon, Police Bureau led to a job as a police recruit. There he discovered that cops were not the bad guys, the criminals were. And he decided to stay a police officer to help the victims of those criminals. Moose rose through the ranks in Portland to become the chief, a position he held for six years. In 1999 he moved to Maryland, where he was hired as chief of the Montgomery County Police Department. Three years later he headed the task force charged with finding the DC Snipers.

In 2003 Moose caused a controversy with his plan to write a book about the DC Sniper case. Critics complained that he was trying to profit from tragedy. Moose resigned as chief on June 28, 2003; his book, *Three Weeks in October*, was published later that year.

reported sightings of what people thought was the sniper's van. Police officers in Montgomery and surrounding counties stopped and searched hundreds of suspect vehicles while their drivers were handcuffed and held at gunpoint. "We were dizzy by all the white box trucks going by," one officer later remarked, "some with signs and markings, some without."[12]

Throughout the afternoon of October 3, law enforcement officials were busy combing the crime scenes for clues, interviewing possible witnesses, and fielding telephone tips about white box trucks. By 9:15 P.M. it had been almost twelve hours since Lori Ann Lewis-Rivera, the latest victim, had been gunned down. Could the sniper finally have ended his rampage? The answer to that unspoken question came with the ringing of a phone at Montgomery County police headquarters. Another shooting had taken place, this time in the nation's capital itself.

Death on a Street Corner

The victim of the latest shooting was seventy-two-year-old Pascal Charlot, a Haitian immigrant who liked to take daily strolls around his Washington, DC, neighborhood. A retired carpenter who enjoyed gardening and helping his neighbors, especially with fix-it projects, Charlot was the father of five and a devoted husband to his wife, who was suffering from Alzheimer's disease. During his walk on the night of October 3, he stood on the corner of Georgia Avenue and Kalmia Road, preparing to cross the street. Then, as had happened so many times that day, a shot suddenly rang out. Charlot crumpled to the sidewalk, bleeding from a bullet wound in his chest. Several passersby and a police officer tried to help him, but his condition was too grave. An ambulance soon arrived in response to a 911 call, but less than an hour later the day's last victim died at a local hospital.

At the crime scene just moments after the fatal shot was fired, a dark colored car with tinted windows pulled onto Kalmia Road and headed west with its headlights off. About

Family members attend the funeral of Pascal Charlot, the sixth sniper victim to die.

an hour later an officer on his way to work at the Prince George's County Police Department noticed the same car driving in a suspicious manner along the Beltway, a heavily traveled freeway that encircles the nation's capital. The officer noted that the license plates were from New Jersey, and typed the number—NDA-21Z—into his computer. No information came back on the computer screen: The car was not stolen, nor was it linked to any crime. As the officer proceeded on to his job, the car with the tinted windows drove off toward Virginia.

On October 3, 2002, in a span of less than fourteen hours, five innocent people had been brutally gunned down. With the killing of James Martin the day before, it all added up to a major crime spree being perpetrated by an unknown serial killer. The citizens of greater Washington, DC, now lived in the shadow of fear, because the randomness of the shootings meant anyone could be the sniper's next victim. Law enforcement authorities were taxed to the limit by the multiple crime scenes, and frustrated by the lack of eyewitnesses and the apparent lack of clues. But there were clues, even at this early stage of the investigation. They were hidden inside the victims themselves, and it was the job of forensic scientists to find them.

CHAPTER 2

Bullets and a Telltale Card

Forensics is the use of science and technology to discover evidence at a crime scene and determine the value of that evidence for use in a civil or criminal trial. Every criminal leaves some evidence at a crime scene. Many clues are obvious, such as footprints, tire tracks, or weapons. Other clues are hidden, and it takes experts to discover them. These forensic scientists include skilled people from many disciplines, including fingerprint experts, weapons specialists, chemical and electronics experts, and medical examiners. In the DC Sniper case, the first forensic scientists called upon were medical experts.

On Friday morning, October 4, 2002, Dr. David R. Fowler, chief medical examiner for the state of Maryland, gathered his staff in the autopsy room of the Office of the Chief Medical Examiner (OCME) facility on Penn Street in downtown Baltimore. Despite being housed in an aging building with limited space and poor ventilation, the OCME routinely performed some eight thousand death investigations and three thousand autopsies a year. This day's examinations were especially important, because they included several victims of the sniper attacks. Police officials, anxious to begin collecting evidence in the sniper case, had wanted Fowler to begin the autopsies the night before. But Fowler, a stickler for following proper procedure, insisted on waiting until morning, when his team would be fresh and rested.

X-rays of the victims' bodies had been taken, however, and these films were now displayed on illuminated viewing boxes in the autopsy room. Deputy chief medical examiner Dr. Mary Ripple noted a particular pattern on some of the X-rays. Each victim had been killed by a single bullet; this much the investigators already knew. What these X-rays revealed was a pattern of tiny flecks that spread out from the entrance wound in the body, indicating that the bullet had fragmented on impact. Since bullets are generally made of a lead alloy, a material that is opaque to X-rays, the fragments were white, giving the appearance of scattered snowflakes on the films. This pattern is referred to by forensic pathologists as a lead snowstorm, and it can give an indication of the type of weapon used by a shooter.

Just as there are numerous types of weapons, from small concealable pistols to high-powered rifles, there is also a wide range of bullets that can be fired by these weapons. What is commonly referred to as a bullet is more accurately termed

The History of Firearm Identification

Firearm identification was probably first used in a case in 1835 in London, England. After a man was murdered, police examined the lead ball projectile and were able to match marks on it to the mold in which it was made. This and other evidence helped pinpoint the victim's servant as the killer. During the Civil War, Confederate general Stonewall Jackson was shot and killed on the battlefield. Examination of the bullet removed from Jackson's body revealed that the fatal shot had come from one of his own troops.

As weapons began incorporating rifling (spiral grooves) in the barrel, new techniques emerged. In 1912 a French professor devised a method of using photographs to compare marks on evidence bullets with marks on test-fired bullets. He also used this technique to examine cartridge casing markings. In the United States, the Bureau of Forensic Ballistics was established in 1925 to provide firearms identification services to law enforcement agencies nationwide. The bureau pioneered the use of the comparison microscope for examining bullets, ushering in the modern era of forensic firearm identification.

a cartridge. Cartridges are made up of two parts: a lead bullet or slug, (the projectile itself), and a copper shell casing that contains the explosive gunpowder that propels the bullet out of the barrel of the weapon. In most modern cartridges the lead projectile is covered, either partially or completely, with a copper sheath, or jacket. Fully sheathed slugs, known as full metal jacket, allow deep penetration of a target and usually exit the victim intact. In partially sheathed bullets, called jacketed soft point or jacketed hollow point, the lead tip is left exposed, allowing the slug to deform on impact. This type of bullet breaks apart inside the target, scattering lead and copper fragments in the victim's body and causing massive trauma. On an X-ray, these fragments display the kind of pattern that Ripple's team saw.

Since no one spotted a shooter in the vicinity of any of the victims, it was safe to assume the murder weapon was not a handgun. The sniper most likely used a rifle to carry out his killing spree. This assumption was supported by the autopsies performed on the victims. The small entrance wounds and massive internal damage observed during the postmortem examinations indicated that the murder weapon was a high-powered rifle. To determine just what kind of rifle was used, law enforcement officials turned to an expert source: the Bureau of Alcohol, Tobacco and Firearms (ATF).

In the Lab

The Bureau of Alcohol, Tobacco and Firearms was officially established in 1972 to "conduct criminal investigations, regulate the firearms and explosives industries, and assist other law enforcement agencies."[13] (In 2003 the agency was transferred from the Treasury Department to the Department of Homeland Security, and the word "Explosives" was added to its name.) In a fortunate coincidence, in 2002 the ATF's National Laboratory Center was located in Rockville, Maryland, not far from Montgomery County police headquarters. When the numerous bullet fragments were removed

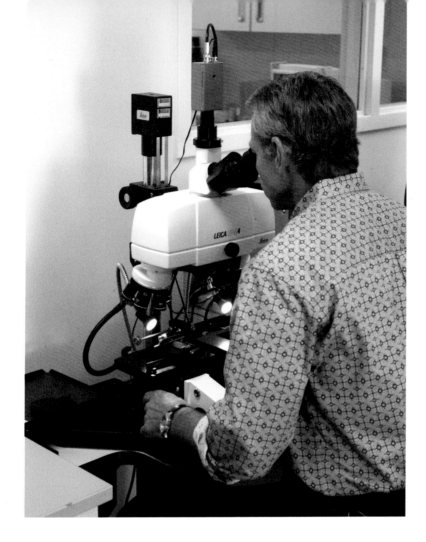

A forensic scientist examines bullets under a comparison microscope to determine whether they were fired by the same gun.

from the sniper victims' bodies during the autopsies, they were quickly delivered to the ATF lab.

Once at the lab, the fragments came under the scrutiny of agent Walter A. Dandridge Jr. An expert in firearms identification, Dandridge placed the tiny pieces of lead and copper under the lenses of a comparison microscope. Ordinarily, the investigator's job is made easier if there is a complete slug to work with. An intact slug, even if damaged by impact, can be microscopically compared with a bullet fired from a known weapon. All weapons leave unique marks, or striations, on the bullets they fire; if these marks match under the microscope, the examiner knows that the slugs were fired from the same weapon.

Although Dandridge had only fragments to work with, he could still draw some conclusions about the bullets and the

Performing a Ballistics Test

1 **A test bullet is fired** from the suspect weapon into a water tank.

2 **The test bullet is recovered** and placed into one side of a comparison microscope.

3 **The bullet from the crime scene** is placed in the other side of the microscope and the images are aligned.

4 **The bullets are turned** in order to try to match the markings left on them from the rifling (grooves) in the barrel of the suspect weapon.

5 **If a match is made,** it indicates that the test and crime scene bullets came from the same weapon.

6 **In a similar manner,** shell casings can be compared to find matches in marks made by the firing pin and breech face (the rear end of the barrel through which the firing pin protrudes).

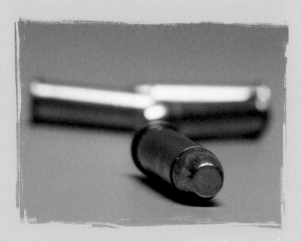

Ballistics tests are used to identify markings on a bullet or shell casing to determine if a suspect weapon fired the projectile.

weapon that fired them. He was able to determine that the bullets fired by the sniper were .223 caliber ammunition. Caliber refers to the diameter of the bullet, so the sniper's slug was slightly less than .25 inch (6.35mm) in diameter. This confirmed suspicions held by Moose and other investigators of the sniper's use of a high-powered rifle. Unfortunately for the investigators, the .223 caliber bullet is one of the most common types of ammunition for both military and civilian use. Dozens of weapons use .223 caliber ammunition, and law enforcement officials had to narrow down the list. While the investigation was going on, however, the DC Sniper struck again.

Victim Number Seven

On Friday, October 4, Caroline Seawell got into her tan Toyota minivan and went shopping at the Spotsylvania Towne Centre in Fredericksburg, Virginia. At around 2:30 that afternoon, the forty-three-year-old homemaker and mother of two left a Michaels craft store across the parking lot from the mall and began loading her purchases—Halloween decorations, including a wreath and a scarecrow—into the van. Suddenly a shot rang out as a stunned Seawell stood by her van. At breakfast that morning, she had discussed the sniper shootings with her husband. Now, Caroline Seawell had become the latest victim.

"I knew that I had been shot immediately," Seawell later recalled. "I first prayed—first said a prayer that God wouldn't let me die. And then I said I was shot."[14] As she collapsed to the ground several bystanders, including a sheriff's deputy, rushed to her aid until paramedics arrived. Although Seawell was in critical condition with injuries to her liver and diaphragm and massive internal bleeding, a quick trip to the hospital saved her life. At the crime scene, investigators looking for clues discovered a gouge in the back of the Toyota van, indicating that the bullet had passed through Seawell's body. Officers examined the van and located the damaged bullet, which they immediately sent by helicopter to Dandridge at the ATF lab. As investigators scoured the scene for additional clues, almost lost was the fact that a dark-colored car with tinted windows and the New Jersey license plate number NDA-21Z had been seen in the Spotsylvania Towne Centre parking lot around the time of the shooting.

The shooting of Caroline Seawell appeared to be the start of a new phase in the sniper shootings. The first six killings all had taken place in the congested suburbs within a few miles of the center of Washington, DC. Seawell was shot in Fredericksburg, Virginia, a mostly rural community more than 50 miles (80.5km) south of the other crime scenes. Investigators now had even more unanswered questions. Was the sniper starting to expand his territory, perhaps into a nationwide crime spree? Where would he strike next? Was the fact that this latest shooting had taken place near a Michaels craft store of any

Caroline Seawell, the seventh victim of the DC Snipers, was shot in the abdomen but survived her injuries.

Building the Joint Operations Center

As the sniper-victim count mounted, more office space was needed to handle the growing investigation. A building next to the Montgomery County Police Department headquarters was leased for a joint operations center, or JOC, described here in an official report:

Encompassing an open space of some 5,000 square feet [464.5 sq. m] on three levels, the building was divided into different workspaces. This task was accomplished in just over 24 hours. . . . The FBI agreed to pay for the building rental, tables and equipment, including projection screens, fax machines and telephones. Miles of telephone line and computer cable were strung from the ceilings. Nextel donated cell phones with walkie-talkie functions. The FBI and ATF contributed substantial resources and equipment for the JOC. . . . The ATF provided a server that held all of the data collected from the case and acquired a satellite television system to monitor media coverage. In four days, the Sniper Task Force went from cramped hallways to a relatively spacious office building. Within just one week, however, the task force realized that even 5,000 square feet was not enough space.

Quoted in Chuck Wexler, Gerard M. Murphy, and Heather J. Davies, *Managing a Multijurisdictional Case: Identifying the Lessons Learned from the Sniper Investigation.* Washington, DC: Police Executive Research Forum, 2004, p. 52.

importance? Since the sniper's first bullet had smashed through the window of a Michaels in Aspen Hill, Maryland, perhaps the craft store chain was somehow connected to the shootings.

At a press conference that evening, an ATF official confirmed that the bullet taken from Seawell's van matched the fragments from four of the six earlier shootings, positively linking the attacks. Then a frustrated Moose made a desperate plea to the sniper as the TV cameras rolled: "Whoever is involved

in this madness, rethink what you're doing. Turn yourself in. Surrender to law enforcement."[15] He also announced that there was a $50,000 reward for any information leading to the arrest of the DC Sniper (the reward eventually grew to $500,000).

The weekend of October 5 and 6 was quiet, with no further sniper attacks. But it was not a time of relaxation for law enforcement. Officers worked tirelessly to begin setting up the investigative infrastructure that would be needed for the DC Sniper case. The command bus had proved so crowded and unreliable that the operation was moved into Montgomery County police headquarters. But even headquarters soon became too cramped and eventually space in a building next door was converted into a joint operations center (JOC) to accommodate the task force that was coordinating the growing investigation. The task force included personnel from the FBI, ATF, U.S. Marshals, and local, county, and state law enforcement agencies.

While the JOC was being set up, Moose kept reporters informed of the progress of the case. At a Saturday press conference he stated for the first time that there were probably two people involved in the sniper shootings: "My experience," he announced, "would say you got a driver, you got a shooter."[16] But the identity of the suspect or suspects remained a mystery.

A reporter asked the chief what was being done to protect the citizens of Montgomery County, especially children, who were vulnerable when going to and from school. "I pointed out to them," Moose later wrote, "that we had posted officers in front of schools. What I didn't tell them was that this was probably accomplishing nothing. . . . I didn't know if having them there was any kind of deterrent at all. I thought it probably wasn't."[17] The sniper soon proved that Moose's doubts were correct.

The Youngest Victim

As the weekend turned to Monday and the JOC began to function, there was an air of optimism in Montgomery County. No one had been shot over the weekend, and the latest victim, Caroline Seawell, was still alive. People were going about their normal weekly routines: beginning the commute to work, getting a head start on their household chores, or driving their kids to school. It was a quiet morning outside Benjamin Tasker Middle School in Bowie, Maryland. The school did not officially open until 8:30 A.M., but shortly after 8:00 a few early students had begun arriving at the beige brick school building. One of those students was thirteen-year-old Iran Brown.

Iran's aunt, Tanya Brown, drove him to school that Monday morning. At 8:09 A.M. she pulled up in front of the school and Iran got out, grabbed his backpack, and headed for the building. As Tanya pulled away from the curb, a loud bang rang out and Iran crumpled to the ground. "Aunt Tanya!" he screamed. A teacher who had been standing nearby rushed to the boy's side. "I've been shot," he told her.[18] By this time, Tanya Brown had backed her car up to where she had dropped Iran off moments before. Iran shakily stood up, and she could see blood spreading on his white shirt from a wound in his chest. As a nurse, Tanya realized that her nephew was severely injured and that she had to act quickly. After buckling Iran into the front passenger seat, Tanya sped off, heading toward a nearby clinic while at the same time dialing 911 on her cell phone.

At the clinic, the Bowie Health Center, doctors examined Iran and determined that his injuries were more severe than

Iran Brown, aged thirteen, was the youngest person to be shot by the DC Snipers.

they could handle. X-rays revealed the snowstorm pattern of high-power bullet fragments, which had damaged Iran's stomach, pancreas, spleen, and lung. Iran was stabilized and then flown by helicopter to Washington's Children's Hospital, where surgeons fought to save the teen's life.

Meanwhile, the crime scene at Tasker Middle School swarmed with investigators, including busloads of police recruits from the Montgomery County Police Academy. A wooded area across the street from the school seemed a likely place from which the sniper might have taken his shot. The recruits scoured the area looking for bullet fragments, spent cartridges, or anything else that might provide a clue to the identity of the shooter. The U.S. Marshals Service brought in dogs trained to sniff out traces of explosives such as gunpowder, and the canines began to hunt for evidence in the dense underbrush. Before long they discovered an area that led to the first real break in the case.

The area was about 150 yards (137m) from the front of Tasker Middle School, and was matted down as if someone

Iran Brown's classmates at Tasker Middle School gathered hundreds of get-well cards for the injured teen.

Becoming an ATF Special Agent

Job Description:
ATF special agents investigate criminal violation of federal laws relating to explosives, firearms, arson, and violations of alcohol and tobacco laws. They gather and analyze evidence, prepare reports, and testify for the government in court.

Education:
A bachelor's degree (or equivalent experience) is required for the entry-level position. Superior academic achievement or an advanced degree will qualify candidates for advanced pay grades.

Qualifications:
ATF applicants must be U.S. citizens between the ages of twenty-one and thirty-seven. They must pass an interview and a series of tests, including a physical test, medical examination, a polygraph test, and drug screening.

Additional Information:
Applicants must be legally able to carry a firearm (that is, they may not have been convicted of a felony or certain misdemeanors that prohibit eligibility for firearm possession) and must be willing to relocate to any ATF office in the United States.

Salary:
Base pay of $31,075 to $39,448 per year, plus a 25 percent increase due to the nature of law enforcement work, and an additional percentage depending on work location.

had been hiding there, perhaps waiting for a potential victim to appear in the sights of a high-powered rifle. In the underbrush officers found an empty .223 caliber shell casing and part of a ballpoint pen. Then, about 25 feet (7.6m) from the casing, someone spotted what looked like a playing card on the ground. It was not an ordinary card, however, but a tarot card, the kind used in fortune-telling and other occult activities. Ominously, the card was the death card, depicting a skeleton wearing armor, holding a flag, and riding a white horse. On the front of the card, hand printed in blue ink, were the words "Call me God." The reverse had three lines written on it: "For you Mr. Police," "Code: Call me God," and "Do not release to the Press." Moose later called the tarot card "the first piece of hard evidence in the whole case. This was the first communication we had with the sniper."[19]

Tarot Card Analysis

Authorities wondered, if this was indeed an attempt by the sniper to communicate with them, what the killer was trying to say. They also pondered how to respond. Moose decided that they should not release details of the card to the press, just as the sniper had demanded. He was afraid that a mention of the card in the media might suggest that he was ignoring the sniper's wishes, and could jeopardize any chance of creating a dialogue with the sniper. At a press conference later that Monday, Moose made a tentative overture toward the sniper. Without mentioning the tarot card, Moose spoke directly to the TV cameras, saying, "I hope to *God*" he said, "that someday we'll know why all this has occurred."[20] By emphasizing the word "God," Moose hoped the sniper would realize that the card had been found and that he was trying to establish communication. Now all he could do was wait for a reply.

The clues found in the woods across from the school were sent to labs for analysis. The ballpoint pen barrel could be tested for DNA, and the marks on the .223 shell casing made by its weapon's firing pin and extractor (the mechanism that ejects the shell from the rifle) were to be microscopically examined. The tarot card itself was not worth much as physical evidence. Its condition told investigators that no fingerprints or DNA could be taken from it, and there was no way to trace where it had been purchased. The only unique feature was the handwritten inscriptions, and the handwriting as well as the ink were analyzed.

Rapid Start

While Moose waited for a response to his press conference message to the sniper, he received some bad news. Both a local television station and the *Washington Post* had leaked information about the tarot card. Moose was furious that the card was now

A tarot card similar to this one was found near the scene where Iran Brown was shot.

Performing an Autopsy

In a suspicious or unnatural death an autopsy, or examination of the dead body, is performed to try to determine the cause of death. A typical autopsy takes two to four hours, but can take longer in a complicated case.

1 The body is washed, measured, and weighed. In a homicide case, any physical evidence (such as fibers or gunshot residue) is collected.

2 If deemed necessary, photographs or X-rays are taken.

3 The torso is opened with a Y-shaped incision.

4 Internal organs are removed, weighed, and visually examined. The medical examiner dictates his or her findings into a recorder.

5 If wounds are present, the examiner must determine the type of weapon used. With a gunshot wound, slugs (if any) are collected and the bullet trajectory traced.

6 The skull is opened and the brain removed and examined.

7 Slices of organs are prepared for later microscopic examination.

8 After the autopsy, the body is sewn back up and released to a funeral home.

9 The medical examiner prepares the final autopsy report.

public knowledge, and in a press conference he angrily scolded reporters for their actions. Moose later said the leaked information "brought out every nut in the country. We had to wade through all these false leads."[21] The leads started to come in almost immediately. Police received calls, faxes, and e-mails from people who claimed to be the sniper. They usually included the words "I am God" as an identifying code, echoing the television and newspaper reports, which got the actual phrase "Call me God" incorrect. Other calls came from tarot card experts who offered to solve the case by examining the sniper's card. As the chief had feared, these calls placed a burden on his already overworked officers. "I am . . . certain that the leak of the tarot card slowed down the investigation," Moose says.[22]

In the days following the shooting of Iran Brown, more than six thousand calls were received by the police tip line that had been set up soon after the first sniper attacks. Not knowing which leads were valuable and which were not, law enforcement officials had to investigate each one. To sort through this flood of information, authorities used an FBI computer program called Rapid Start. A case management system, Rapid Start is used to organize leads coming into law enforcement offices. At the joint operations center in Montgomery County, information from lead sheets (notes written by the officers taking the calls) was entered into the Rapid Start computers. The system allowed investigators to keep track of leads, cross-reference information to look for links, and avoid duplication of data. By the morning of October 8, authorities had a few clues and hundreds of telephone tips, but still had no clear picture of their adversary. One Montgomery County police official described the elusive sniper as "a ghost with a gun."[23] Law enforcement personnel were not the only ones speaking out about the sniper. Maryland governor Parris N. Glendening told the press, "We're talking about a person here who is basically a coward. This is not an individual here who is out there doing something strong or manly or anything of this type."[24] These were impassioned words, but at the time no one knew if they were accurate. To try to discover the true nature of the DC Sniper, Moose and his task force turned to an area of forensic science that dealt not with external evidence, but rather with the mind and personality of the killer.

CHAPTER 3

Profile of a Killer

One of the most frightening and frustrating aspects of the DC Sniper shootings was the random nature of the killings. Aside from the fact that each victim was struck by a single bullet from a high-powered rifle, investigators could find no other similarities that might indicate a motive for the shootings. What, they wondered, would cause someone to arbitrarily target such a diverse group of innocent people, including a man mowing a lawn, a woman sitting on a bench, and a thirteen-year-old middle school student? While one group of investigators pored over the physical evidence, another group was working to answer that very question.

How and Why

Located in Quantico, Virginia, the FBI's Behavioral Analysis Unit is the home of the agency's criminal behavior investigators—popularly known as profilers. In a serial murder case such as the DC Sniper shootings, an FBI profiler studies the crime scenes, examines the physical evidence, and analyzes the method and time and place of the killings. The profiler also analyzes the victim: his or her physical characteristics, personality, background, education, and anything the person may have done to motivate the crime. This is a relatively new area of criminal investigation called victimology, and it has become an important part of the profiling process. The profiler may also study previous cases that appear to be similar in nature. Using all this information, the profiler then develops an assessment of the type of person or persons likely to have committed the crime. This assessment (a term the FBI prefers over profile) is then given to the local law enforcement agencies investigating the case. It is generally accepted that profiling is as much, if not more, an art as it is a science. Former FBI profiler John Douglas comments, "I use a formula: How plus Why equals Who. If we can answer the hows and whys in a crime, we generally can come up with the solution."[25]

In the case of the DC Sniper, on October 9 Moose received a ten-page profile report from the FBI's Behavioral Analysis Unit. The special agents who prepared the report, Stephen Etter and Mark Hilts, called their conclusions probabilities, advising Moose that the profile might not completely fit the unknown assailant. Among these probabilities were the following:

> There is likely only one offender. The offender is a male. Historically, cases similar to this series have been perpetrated primarily by white males. The offender will have

A forensic analyst works with computer equipment to examine evidence. The FBI used behavioral analysis to try to determine what kind of person would carry out the sniper shootings.

a definite fascination/interest in weapons. The offender will likely be known to others as an angry person.[26]

While the FBI report was very specific in its probabilities, it alone did not provide enough information on which to base the sniper investigation. "The FBI guys were doing the best they could with the limited information available," Moose later remarked, "but if we had been waiting on them to create a blueprint for our investigation, or a crystal-clear portrait of our killer, we would have been disappointed."[27] Fearing another leak to the press, Moose allowed only a few of his investigators access to the information in the FBI report. There was already no shortage of media speculation. Former police officers and retired profilers appeared on television to present their theories on who the sniper might be. While the TV commentators were discussing the possible identity of the sniper, the killer was planning yet another attack.

Police cars surround the Sunoco gas station in Manassas, Virginia, at which Dean Meyers was shot.

The Killing of Dean Meyers

At around 8:00 P.M. on October 9, Dean Harold Meyers was preparing to begin the long commute home from his office in Manassas, Virginia, where he was a project manager at a civil engineering firm, to his townhouse in Gaithersburg, Maryland. A decorated veteran of the Vietnam War, Meyers was a conscientious employee who often worked long after the office had closed. As he began the forty-mile (64.4km) drive home Meyers noticed that his car needed gas. He pulled the dark gray Mazda into a Sunoco station at the intersection of two busy highways, about half a mile (.8km) from the First Virginia Bank. The evening air was chilly as Meyers stood filling the Mazda's tank under the cold glare of the lights at the top of the pump island. For a skilled sniper, fifty-three-year-old Dean Harold Meyers was a perfect target. It was 8:15 P.M.

Meyers finished fueling the Mazda and was about to get back into the car when the loud crack of a rifle rang out across the pavement of the Sunoco station. Another customer at the station turned at the sound of the shot to see Meyers collapse between the Mazda and the gas pumps. One look told the man that Meyers was critically injured, so he ran to the station office and told an employee to call 911. During the call, the employee mentioned a white van that was seen leaving moments after the shooting. Officers were on the scene within two minutes, but for Meyers it was too late. The soft-spoken veteran who had survived the Vietnam War had been killed in his native country by a sniper's shot to the head.

Encounter with the Snipers

Officer Steven Bailey, a two-year veteran of the Prince William County Police Department, was one of the officers who arrived on the scene in response to the 911 call. Bailey was assigned to interview possible witnesses in the parking lot of the Bob Evans restaurant across the road from the Sunoco station. He pulled his squad car across the exit and began to question

motorists as they left the lot. Driver after driver reported that they had seen nothing suspicious, so Bailey let them go.

One of the cars in the lot was a dark blue Chevrolet Caprice. As it pulled up to Bailey, the driver, an African American man, rolled down his window. The officer could see no one else in the car. Bailey later described the incident: "I asked [the driver] if he had heard or seen anything. He stated he did not. He said he was coming home from vacation . . . and the police directed him into the parking lot. He was very polite and courteous."[28] Like the other motorists Bailey questioned that night, the man appeared to be just another citizen who had not seen anything. Bailey waved the driver through, and the dark blue car with New Jersey license plates rolled off into the night.

Only later did it occur to Bailey that something about the story the driver of the blue Caprice had told him did not quite add up. Why would the police direct cars into a parking lot across the street from the scene of a deadly shooting, with the sniper possibly still around? It just did not make sense, but it was too late to do anything about it now; the car was long gone. "I didn't catch on," Bailey later commented. "I wish I had."[29]

Unknown to Bailey, the driver of the dark blue Caprice was a man named John Allen Muhammad, although throughout his life he had used a dozen aliases, including Wayne Weeks, James Edwards, and his real birth name, John Allen Williams. Also in the car was a seventeen-year-old Jamaican youth named Lee Boyd Malvo. While law enforcement authorities were spending thousands of man-hours looking for white box trucks and a lone white sniper, Muhammad and Malvo were, in fact, the DC Snipers, cruising the Washington, DC, area in the blue Caprice and shooting innocent victims at random.

The Manipulator

At various times in his life, John Allen Muhammad was described as trustworthy, a good father, and "the person you looked up to and wanted to be like."[30] But he had a dark side as well. "My father was a manipulator," says Lindbergh Williams, Muhammad's oldest son. "If he sees a weakness, he'll take advantage."[31]

Born in New Orleans on the last day of 1960, John Allen Williams (he later changed his name to Muhammad as part of his conversion to Islam) had a difficult early life. His father was seldom around, and after his mother died of cancer when John was three, he went to live with two aunts and a domineering grandfather. Quiet and introverted, John was a loner during his school years. After high school he joined the Louisiana Army National Guard, and there, amid the crisp

John Allen Muhammad suffered a difficult childhood and had conflicts with other soldiers while he was in the military.

Trouble in the Army

John Allen Muhammad's service to his country in the army was plagued with problems and accusations. Then known as John Williams, he served in Saudi Arabia during the Persian Gulf War in 1991. While overseas with an engineering unit, Muhammad was involved in racial clashes with several of his fellow soldiers, as well as some other minor conflicts such as using another soldier's sleeping bag. His angry reactions to being reprimanded made his comrades wary of his temper.

A more serious incident occurred one night when Muhammad was accused of igniting an incendiary grenade in a tent where soldiers were sleeping. The burning grenade set off ammunition in the tent, but all the occupants escaped safely. Muhammad, who had earlier had a run-in with one of the soldiers, was arrested by the military police. The facts of the case were not clear, however, and Muhammad was never charged with the crime. But the sergeant who accused him was so sure that Muhammad would some day seek revenge that he carried a piece of paper with the name Williams on it, just in case something should happen to him.

uniforms and military discipline, he found a sense of belonging. In 1985 he joined the regular army, gaining skills in engineering and marksmanship. He became a Sharpshooter (a mid-grade achievement between Marksman and Expert) with the standard military M-16 rifle. Williams served in the Persian Gulf War, but his military career was marred by a series of run-ins with other soldiers.

After leaving the army, Muhammad set up an auto mechanic business with his wife, Mildred, in Tacoma, Washington. He had three children with Mildred (Lindbergh was John's son from a previous marriage), but the couple separated in September 1999 due to Mildred's accusations that John abused her. The marriage eventually ended in divorce.

Afterward, Muhammad's life seemed to begin a downward spiral of anger and despair. Mildred filed for an order of protection against her ex-husband after receiving threats, reporting that Muhammad had told her, "You are not going to raise my children. . . . You have become my enemy, and as my enemy, I will kill you."[32] On March 27, 2000, on the pretense of taking his children shopping, Muhammad fled with them to the Caribbean island of Antigua. Mildred did not see her children again for more than a year.

Muhammad's New "Son"

In Antigua, Muhammad took an assumed name and enrolled his children in a local school. He made money by selling forged documents—birth certificates, passports, and identity cards—that allowed people to enter the United States illegally. Among the many people Muhammad helped was a single mother named Una James. James had lived a life of hardship, moving from island to island in the Caribbean to find work, often leaving her son, Lee, behind. She had long dreamed of going to the United States to escape poverty; that dream was fulfilled when she met Muhammad in Antigua. Muhammad supplied forged documents for James and her teenage son to travel to Florida. James left first, leaving her son behind once again. This time, however, Lee had someone to take care of him.

Muhammad was a father figure to Lee Boyd Malvo (pictured).

Lee Boyd Malvo was born in Jamaica on February 18, 1985. He had never known a stable family life. His father, Leslie Malvo, and mother, Una James, split up when Lee was five years old. Despite the hardships, Lee was a quiet, well-mannered child who loved drawing and playing the British game of cricket. But the lack of a father in his life left him craving attention, especially from older men. After James left

Antigua for Florida, fifteen-year-old Lee moved in with Muhammad and his children. Muhammad became the father figure Lee had been seeking, and soon the teen was calling Muhammad "Dad." Without his strict mother to guide him, however, Lee began to change. His schoolwork suffered, and he started practicing the religion of Islam—a surprising conversion for a boy raised in the Seventh-Day Adventist Church.

Muhammad, his three children, and Lee Boyd Malvo left Antigua for good in May 2001. Lee joined his mother in Fort Myers, Florida, while Muhammad took his children to Bellingham, Washington. For a while Lee lived with James in Fort Myers and even enrolled in high school there. But their reunion did not last long; Lee found that he missed being with Muhammad. In early October, James frantically called a friend. "I can't find my son," she said. "I've been looking everywhere."[33]

Lee Boyd Malvo's father, Leslie Malvo (left), and his son Rohan read an article about the DC sniper shootings that was published in a Jamaican newspaper.

She did not know that Lee had boarded a Greyhound bus and was traveling more than 3,300 miles (5,300km) across the United States to Bellingham.

At the Lighthouse

In August 2001 Muhammad and his children had taken up residence at a homeless shelter, the Lighthouse Mission in Bellingham. He registered the children for school and signed up for public assistance. But his illegal abduction of the three children soon caught up with him. When his public aid application was run through a computer database, the order of protection Mildred had filed against him turned up. Authorities realized that Muhammad had illegally taken his children, and obtained a court order to return them to Mildred. At a hearing in Tacoma, Washington, the court awarded Mildred full custody of the children. Although he maintained a calm outward appearance at the decision, Muhammad seethed with anger inside.

By the Numbers

4,000,000

Number of assault rifles owned in the United States

In late October Muhammad returned to the Lighthouse Mission, this time accompanied by Lee Malvo, who he said was his son. From the beginning of their stay at the shelter, Muhammad seemed to exert a strong influence on the impressionable Malvo, and could silence the teenager with a single glare. Reverend Al Archer, head of the mission, noticed his workers were suspicious of Muhammad. "Our staff had the feeling that he [Malvo] was being pulled along by John into something really too big for him,"[34] says Archer.

For the next ten months, Muhammad and Malvo were inseparable, keeping mostly to themselves. "They were always apart from everyone else," recalls mission manager Rory Reublin. "I can't remember Lee Malvo ever talking to anyone else."[35] Muhammad was restless, and he and Malvo drifted across the country by bus, ending up in such places as Tucson,

The Bushmaster

The Bushmaster XM15-E2S is the civilian version of the Colt AR-15, which is used by the U.S. military under the designation M-16. It is named for a highly venomous South American snake and it can be just as deadly. It is a semiautomatic weapon, meaning it fires one round, or bullet, each time the trigger is pulled and then automatically chambers a round for the next shot. The Bushmaster fires a .223 caliber round, which is just less than .25 inch (6.35mm) in diameter, and comes with a standard magazine that holds ten rounds (although larger magazines can accommodate up to one hundred rounds).

The Bushmaster is a lightweight rifle, weighing about 8.2 pounds (3.7kg). There are numerous accessories that allow the Bushmaster to be modified in many different ways; these include optical and electronic sights, night-vision scopes, a fold-up bipod, handgrips, and carrying handles and slings. The Bushmaster is a popular rifle for small-game hunters and target shooters. While it is not usually a sniper's weapon, the events of October 2002 show that in the wrong hands it can also be used for that lethal purpose.

Pictured is the Bushmaster rifle the DC Snipers used to shoot their victims.

Phoenix, Denver, Albuquerque, El Paso, and other cities in the western United States. Back in Washington State in August 2002, they often traveled between Bellingham and Tacoma. While in Tacoma, they frequented a gun shop called Bull's Eye Shooter Supply. Prominently displayed in the store was a recently acquired Bushmaster XM15-E2S semiautomatic rifle, serial number L284320. It was the civilian version of the military M-16 assault rifle and fired .223 caliber ammunition. John Allen Muhammad had earned his Sharpshooter badge with this type of weapon, but could not legally own one because of the order of protection against him. Sometime in August or September 2002, the gun was stolen from the weapons store.

CHAPTER 4

A Message from the Snipers

Muhammad and Malvo were doing a good job of hiding from the authorities. Like many criminals, however, they had a need to boast about their crimes. The tarot card left at the scene of the Iran Brown shooting was their first attempt at communicating with the authorities, but the message was too cryptic to mean anything to the police. While they were pondering other means of communication, the snipers continued their killing spree.

Kenneth H. Bridges, a fifty-three-year-old businessman from Philadelphia, was on his way home from a work meeting on Friday, October 11, 2002. Needing gas, he pulled his rented car off the interstate and into an Exxon station near Massaponax, Virginia, about 50 miles (80.4km) south of Washington, DC. Nearby, a Virginia state trooper was at the scene of a minor traffic accident a mere 50 yards (45.7m) from the station. At about 9:30 A.M. a shot pierced the sounds of the traffic on the interstate. Bridges clutched his chest and managed a few steps before slumping to the ground by the gas pumps. Hearing the shot, the trooper ran to help, but to no avail; Bridges died at a hospital 3 miles (4.8km) from the shooting.

Once again the law enforcement investigation went into action. The grounds of the Exxon station were checked for shell casings, bullet fragments, and any other clues the sniper might have left behind. Police shut down lanes on the interstate and stopped white box vans by the hundreds, causing massive traffic jams. But the perimeter around the gas station had not been closed soon enough. Muhammad and Malvo had slipped through. Two days later they were spending a quiet Sunday afternoon at a YMCA in Burlington, North Carolina.

It was ten days into the shooting spree, and the police still had little to go on. Despite the tarot card and the various bullet fragments, the lack of evidence at the crime scenes left investigators frustrated and angry. A meeting of top law enforcement officers at the University of Maryland was a tense affair. The officers wondered whether more could be done to catch the snipers. Was the obsessive emphasis on finding a white box truck, which so far had turned up nothing, preventing officers from pursuing other avenues of investigation? Four days before, the Washington, DC, Metropolitan Police had issued a "be on the lookout" (BOLO) notification for a dark-colored Chevrolet Caprice observed leaving one of the shooting scenes. Why was this not being given as much attention as the white truck? "I think there's been more law enforcement focus on that," Moose told a TV interviewer when asked later about the car, "[but] not a big push for public feedback about that. . . . The puzzle has yet to come together."[36]

Investigators in Fredericksburg, Virginia, painstakingly look for evidence near the Exxon gas station where the snipers claimed their tenth victim.

While authorities were questioning their own investigative methods, on the evening of Monday, October 14, 2002—Columbus Day—Ted and Linda Franklin shopped at the Home Depot store near Falls Church, Virginia. The store and its two-level parking garage were located at the Seven Corners Shopping Center. A little after 9:00 P.M. the Franklins left the store, pushing a loaded shopping cart toward their red Mercury, which was parked on the lower level of the lot.

Murder at Home Depot

Across the street from the Home Depot parking garage, a dark Chevrolet Caprice with New Jersey license plate number NDA-21Z sat unnoticed in a dimly lit parking area. Anyone who walked by and took notice might have seen the barrel of a rifle sticking out from a hole cut in the trunk of the car. But no one did. Inside the trunk, the killer peered through the rifle's holographic sight. As he steadied his weapon, several people unsuspectingly walked through the aiming point depicted in the scope's small illuminated screen. The sniper knew that someone would die tonight; the only decision left was who it would be.

Ted and Linda Franklin reached their car and began loading their purchases into the trunk. For a moment they struggled with a large item, trying to fit it into the trunk of the small car. They had no idea that across the street, the sniper who had garnered so much publicity in the newspapers and on television for nearly two weeks was drawing a bead on them. It was 9:15 P.M.

The sniper placed the holographic crosshair on Ted Franklin and held his breath for the shot. But the target was moving around too much, making it difficult for the sniper to hold him in the sight. He could take the shot, but a kill might not be guaranteed. The sniper moved his rifle ever so slightly until Linda Franklin came into view, the crosshair settling on her head. She was standing still, a perfect target. Taking another breath, Lee Boyd Malvo squeezed the trigger.

Ted Franklin heard the shot, and when he turned around he saw his wife lying on the ground. Malvo's shot had been perfect; Linda Franklin died instantly. Ted frantically called 911 and within minutes, police cars began descending on the scene. Before long, hundreds of FBI, ATF, and other officials had arrived at the Home Depot and were looking for evidence and possible witnesses. At one point later that evening, a detective gave FBI special agent Kevin Lewis some distressing news: Linda Franklin worked as an analyst for the FBI. The DC Snipers had now felled one of law enforcement's own.

Some 2,800 miles (4,500km) away in Tacoma, Washington, Robert Holmes watched the television coverage of the killing of Linda Franklin. Holmes, who worked as an auto mechanic, was an army veteran. He had seen news reports of the other sniper killings, but this one seemed to confirm a hunch that

Shopping for a Killing Machine

John Muhammad wanted to buy a car, supposedly for his so-called son Lee Malvo. When he and Malvo arrived by bus in Camden, New Jersey, on September 10, 2002, he called on twenty-six-year-old Nathaniel Osbourne, the brother of an old friend. Osbourne took pity on the scruffy twosome, so he gave them something to eat and then took them car shopping. After passing up several small foreign cars, Muhammad saw the one he wanted at a used car lot in Trenton, New Jersey. It was a rather beat-up 1990 Chevrolet Caprice, but it had what Muhammad was looking for: a large trunk. Osbourne, unaware of what Muhammad had in mind for the Caprice, cosigned for the car, which cost a mere $250. Muhammad now had the killing machine he needed.

In a strange twist of fate, it turned out that the Caprice was a former police cruiser. And compounding the irony of the situation was the name of the used car lot: Sure Shot Auto Sales.

he had. One of his former army buddies was a man he knew as John Allen Williams. On several recent occasions, Williams had stayed at Holmes's house in Tacoma, bringing with him a teenager whom John referred to as "Sniper." Williams and the young man had done some target shooting in Holmes's backyard, pumping bullets from a Bushmaster rifle into an old tree stump. Holmes also knew about Williams's trouble with his ex-wife, who was now living in the Washington, DC, area. After the shooting of Kenneth Bridges on October 11, Holmes had told a friend, "Hey, man, you know, that's John doing that on the East Coast." When his friend expressed disbelief, Holmes simply stated, "It's him. When it's all over and done with you watch."[37] Now, as the story of Linda Franklin's death played out on TV, Holmes thought maybe he should call the FBI tip line. But it was another three days before he picked up the phone.

Contact

After the Franklin shooting, calls to the FBI tip line streamed in at a rate that sometimes reached nearly one thousand an hour. There were crank calls and calls from well-meaning citizens reporting what they felt was suspicious behavior by a relative or neighbor. Each one had to be checked out.

Because the phone number of the Rockville Police Department had appeared on television, calls poured into headquarters as well. On the morning of Tuesday, October 15, Amy Lefkoff, a fourteen-year veteran of the force, was on duty. "I was bombarded with phone calls," Lefkoff recalls. "They were just pouring in, and every call I got related to [the sniper]."[38]

Sometime between 11:00 and 11:15 A.M., Lefkoff's phone rang again. On the other end was the voice of a young man. "Good morning," the voice said. "Don't say

By the Numbers

2 SQUARE MILLIMETERS

Minimum amount of a bullet fragment useable for ballistic comparison

anything. Just listen. We're the people that are causing the killing in your area. Look on the tarot card. It says, 'Call me God. Do not release to the press.' We have called you three times before, trying to set up negotiations. We have got no response. People have died."[39] Lefkoff told the caller that the Rockville Police were not investigating the case, and that he should call Montgomery County instead. The line suddenly clicked dead as Lee Malvo hung up. Lefkoff later played a tape of the call for her supervisor, who decided it should be sent to the Sniper Task Force.

By Friday, October 18, there had been no more shootings for four days. Every day that passed without another murder left authorities of the Sniper Task Force with an unspoken yet hopeful thought: Perhaps the sniper had had his fill of killing and slipped quietly away. There were two sides to the situation, however. "I wondered," Moose later wrote, "if the sniper was done, and if it was over. If it was, it meant no more killings. But it also meant we might never find the person or persons who had killed nine people and seriously wounded two people already."[40]

The snipers were not finished, however. At about 4:30 P.M. that day, a call came in to Montgomery County police

Robert Holmes (left) testifies at John Allen Muhammad's trial. Muhammad and Malvo stayed at Holmes's Tacoma, Washington, home on several occasions.

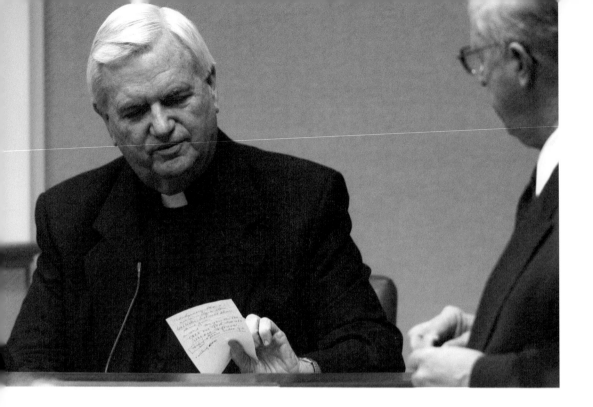

headquarters. Public relations officer Derek Baliles picked up his phone and was greeted by a gruff male voice, most likely that of Malvo: "Shut up and listen, and don't ask any questions."[41]

Baliles obeyed and the caller told him that he had information about the snipers. He also said he would not talk until Baliles looked into a liquor store robbery that took place in Montgomery, Alabama, and involved the shooting of two people. A Sergeant Martino, the caller said, could provide Baliles with details of the crime. During the call, which lasted for three minutes, the caller became increasingly agitated, complaining about the ineptitude of the investigators and finally shouting, "Don't you know who you're dealing with?"[42] More people would die, he said, if the police did not start communicating.

The line suddenly went dead and Baliles sat for a moment, troubled by the caller's menacing tone. Maybe it was only a crank call, but Baliles had to check it out. He called the Montgomery Police Department and was able to track down Sgt. Scott Martino, a detective. Martino confirmed that there had been a liquor store robbery back in September, and that two women, Claudine Parker and Kellie Adams, were shot. Parker had died of her wounds; the killers had escaped. Forensics had found fragments of a .223 caliber bullet, and snowstorm patterns on the victims' X-rays were evidence that a high-powered rifle had been used. Officers also found another clue at the crime scene: a discarded gun catalog. The catalog was bagged and sent to the local police lab, where it was examined for fingerprints. Several prints were found, but they did not match any prints on record in local or state databases, so the catalog was filed away. Baliles wondered what it all meant. He did not realize that Muhammad and Malvo were trying to show that they were experienced killers who desperately wanted to be taken seriously.

Several hours later, Msgr. William Sullivan of St. Ann's Church in Ashland, Virginia, received a call from an agitated young man who began talking about the sniper shootings, ballistics tests, the liquor store robbery, and the tarot card. He said the woman at the Seven Corners Shopping Center did not have to die. The caller was talking fast and Sullivan tried to calm him down, but to no avail. The priest asked, "What do you want me to do?"[43] Malvo told him to contact the police and let them know that the snipers were making telephone calls and that they were serious. Sullivan hung up, convinced he had been talking to a prankster with a vivid imagination. He did not contact the police and soon put the strange call out of his mind.

Muhammad and Malvo were trying to get the attention of the authorities, to flaunt their skill in murdering people at will. But in doing so, they were complicating an already confusing situation. Police phone lines were jammed, and the officers manning the phones were overworked and exhausted. So instead of getting through to the police, the pair got the runaround. The frustrated snipers decided to communicate in the most effective way they could think of: with another killing.

The Letter

Muhammad and Malvo had never before attempted a killing on a weekend. That changed on Saturday, October 19, along with the lives of Stephanie and Jeffrey Hopper. The Hoppers, who lived in Melbourne, Florida, were heading home following a visit to a sick relative in Pennsylvania. As they passed through the Washington, DC, area after several hours of driving, they decided to stop for dinner. The Hoppers knew about the sniper shootings but they assumed that where they were now driving, about 90 miles (145km) south of Washington, was far enough away from danger. They pulled off Interstate 95 toward an area that had a Burger King, an Arby's, and a Ponderosa Steakhouse. They decided to have dinner at the Ponderosa, so Jeff pulled into the restaurant's parking lot. As they parked their car, they could not know that the town they were in, Ashland, was where the snipers' recent phone calls had come from.

ATF agents leave the Ponderosa restaurant in Ashland, Virginia, where Jeff Hopper was shot. Hopper survived his injuries.

After dinner, at about 7:59 P.M., the Hoppers were walking across the Ponderosa parking lot toward their car when they heard a sound like a small explosion. Jeff grabbed his stomach and said, "I've been shot,"[44] as he fell to the ground. Thirty-seven-year-old Hopper was one of the lucky ones; he eventu-

ally survived his wounds after numerous surgeries and a month's stay in the hospital. As with the other shootings, authorities came out in force, blocking roads and checking white trucks—but again ignoring dark-colored Chevrolet Caprices. Wherever Muhammad and Malvo were, they had eluded capture once more. But this time they had left a message for the police.

It was cold, dark, and raining as FBI, ATF, and Hanover County Sheriff's Department officers fanned out in a wooded area that bordered the Ponderosa parking lot. A gunpowder-sniffing dog, led by his trainer, ATF agent Ray Neely, soon discovered a .223 caliber shell casing lying in the underbrush about, 30 feet (9.1m) from the parking lot. Although the casing would have to be examined by ballistics experts to determine if it had been fired from the Bushmaster rifle implicated in the other killings, it was a good indication that the snipers had taken their shot from that spot. As dozens of officers spent the next several hours scouting the area, Deputy Sheriff James Sizemore noticed an object tacked to a tree: a Ziploc bag decorated with Halloween designs and containing what looked like pink papers inside. The bag was carefully removed from the tree and sent to the FBI's DNA Analysis Unit in Quantico to be opened and examined.

Inside the bag the pink papers were found to be a four-page, neatly hand-printed letter from the snipers to police officials. The first page was decorated with five red adhesive stars, and bore some familiar words: "For you mr. Police. 'Call me God.' Do not release to the Press."[45] The writer complained that their telephone calls to various authorities were taken "for a Hoax or Joke, so your failure to respond has cost you five lives. If stopping the killing is more important than catching us now, you will accept our demands which are non-negotiable."[46]

By the Numbers

100,000

Number of calls to the FBI tip line during the DC Sniper spree

FISHing for Clues

The U.S. Secret Service is probably best known for its mission to protect the president of the United States and his family. But the agency also performs many other functions, one of which is document analysis. The Secret Service's Questioned Document Section uses a method called Forensic Information System for Handwriting, or FISH, to analyze and compare writing or hand printing to determine if two documents were written by the same person. Based on the work of German forensic scientists, FISH software works by breaking text into mathematical algorithms. The document analyst scans and digitizes writing samples, which can then be compared to other samples in the FISH database. Currently, the FISH database contains some one hundred thousand writing and printing samples.

An examiner uses the Forensic Information System for Handwriting to compare writing samples.

Their demand was for $10 million to be deposited in a Bank of America Visa credit card account to which the snipers would have unlimited access. The letter further stated that the snipers would contact authorities by calling a pay phone at the Ponderosa at 6:00 A.M. Sunday. And they gave the police until 9:00 A.M. Monday morning to make the $10 million deposit. The letter ended with the snipers promising to keep their side of the bargain and the phrase, "Word is Bond."[47]

Finally, a motive for the shootings was clear: The DC Snipers wanted money. But there were problems. The 6:00 A.M. deadline the snipers had set for contacting police at the Ponderosa had passed before the letter was opened at the FBI lab. Muhammad and Malvo, apparently worried that authorities had not found the letter, called the FBI tip line from Richmond, Virginia, at 9:40 A.M. on Sunday. Again using the code "Call me God" for identification, the caller gave the location of the letter in the woods and said he would call the Ponderosa in ten minutes. But contact was never made.

Muhammad and Malvo were growing more and more desperate to obtain recognition for their crimes. They wanted to prove that they could outsmart the task force and continue to shoot people at will. They failed to realize that each contact was providing information that the police could use to track them down.

CHAPTER 5

Assembling the Puzzle

As the sniper investigation continued, more clues were uncovered by law enforcement authorities. One clue led the police to a false conclusion, while another sent investigators across the country to a backyard in Tacoma, Washington. But the most valuable clues were provided by the snipers themselves: Their attempts to communicate with authorities ultimately revealed their true identities.

Moose learned the details of the new letter on Sunday, October 20. "The discovery of the note," Moose recalls, "was a very dramatic and exciting development. For the first time, we had a motive. We knew what the killing was about. We knew what the killer wanted. We had the beginning of a real negotiation."[48]

But the process of negotiation was becoming a rocky road. With the failure to receive the snipers' call at the Ponderosa on Sunday morning, Moose had to find another way to contact them. Although the snipers had insisted that their communication with law enforcement be kept from the press, there was no way for Moose to reach out to them except through the media. "We had to find a way to communicate with the sniper, without telling the media what we were doing,"[49] Moose says.

The chief began adding cryptic messages to the snipers during some of his press briefings outside the joint operations center. At around 7:00 P.M. on Sunday, Moose stepped before the cameras and microphones and announced: "To the person who left us a message at the Ponderosa Saturday night, you gave us a telephone number. We do want to talk to you. Call us at the number you provided."[50] Negotiators at the joint operations center were waiting to take the call. Officers staked out pay phones across the Ashland area, where the task force speculated the snipers might call from. At just before 8:00 on Monday morning a call came in. It lasted only thirty-eight seconds and the voice, which seemed to be on a tape recording played into the phone, was nearly unintelligible. The call was traced to one of several pay phones near an Exxon gas station outside of Richmond, not far from Ashland. As police cars raced to the scene, officials hoped that this would spell the end of the DC Sniper shooting spree.

False Alarm

Pulling into a car dealership next to the Exxon station, officers surveyed the scene with binoculars. Next to the pay phone where the sniper's call had been traced sat a white Plymouth Voyager van with a male occupant in the driver's seat. Hiding behind cars in the dealer's lot, the officers pulled on bulletproof vests and checked their weapons; by 8:30 all was ready. They

A police officer inspects a van suspected of belonging to the DC Snipers.

The First Victim

The thirteen people killed or wounded in the October 2002 shooting spree were not the only victims of the DC Snipers. Muhammad and Malvo committed their first murder in Tacoma, Washington, almost eight months before their spree began. The killing took place at the home of Isa and Joseph Nichols, a tidy yellow house in the Roosevelt Heights section of Tacoma. Isa had been Muhammad's accountant in his auto repair business, and was a close friend of his ex-wife, Mildred. Muhammad became angry with Isa when she sided with Mildred during the legal battle to regain custody of her three children. Muhammad planned to someday take revenge.

On the evening of February 16, 2002, the doorbell rang at the Nichols home. Alone in the house was twenty-one-year-old Keenya Cook, Isa's niece, who also lived there with her six-month-old daughter. As she cautiously opened the front door and looked out into the darkness, there was a sudden flash and a loud noise. Cook collapsed on the doorstep: a bullet had smashed through her face, killing her instantly. The subsequent investigation turned up no suspects. No one then suspected that Lee Boyd Malvo had fired the fatal shot as the first test of his willingness to kill for John Allen Muhammad. And Isa Nichols did not know how close she came to becoming the first victim of Muhammad's rage.

slowly approached the van, assault rifles aimed at the man in the driver's seat. It took only seconds for the officers to pull the suspect from the van and handcuff him. A second man who was walking near the van was also arrested.

Local television stations and cable news outlets broke into their regular programming with live coverage of the scene. Sitting in his office in Rockville, Moose watched the capture as it unfolded on TV. But something seemed wrong: Why would the sniper, who was being sought by every law enforcement officer in the DC area, hang around a pay phone for a half hour after calling the police? He had to realize the call would be traced. "It's not them,"[51] Moose quietly said.

The two men arrested were Edgar García and José Morales, illegal immigrants from Mexico and Guatemala. They were taken into custody and questioned by police, a difficult task since the two men spoke little English. García, the owner of the van, had apparently picked up a different pay phone than the snipers had used, and was talking while snipers had made their call on another phone and then left the scene. After determining that the men were not the snipers, police turned them over to the Immigration and Naturalization Service (INS). García and Morales were soon on their way back to their native countries. Although police knew they had missed the real snipers, they had no idea how close they had come. In fact, as the capture was playing out before a nationwide television audience, Muhammad and Malvo were just a short distance away, calmly watching the arrest of Morales and García.

"A Duck in a Noose"

Shortly after 10:00 A.M. Moose held a press briefing in which he tried to assure the snipers that authorities were still working on communicating with them. "We are going to respond to a message that we have received," Moose said. "We will respond later. We are preparing our response at this time."[52] That preparation included trying to decipher what the voice in the latest phone call had said.

The voice was that of a young man with an accent. After repeating the familiar code, "Call me God," the caller made a strange request: "You will hold a press conference, stating to the media that you believe you have caught the

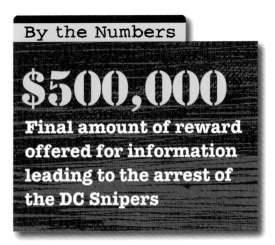

By the Numbers

$500,000

Final amount of reward offered for information leading to the arrest of the DC Snipers sniper like a duck in a noose. Repeat every word exactly as you heard it."[53]

Officers had never heard the peculiar phrase before, and began trying to track down its meaning. Others tried to determine the origin of the caller's accent, and decided that he probably came from the Caribbean area, possibly from Jamaica. Two U.S. marshals on the task force, both experts in Jamaican gangs, now began making connections. A computer search found that the phrase "Word is bond," which appeared in the Ponderosa letter, was included in the lyrics of a rap song performed by several groups, including a reggae band. The song began, "Word is bond./Pop pop pop pop/Grab your chest. Now ya bleeding. . . ."[54] Other phrases used by the snipers, "Call me God" and "Mr. Police," also turned up as rap lyrics.

The cryptic "duck in a noose" reference was found to have come from a Cherokee folktale about a rabbit who tries unsuccessfully to capture a duck in a noose. But what did the snipers mean by including this phrase in their message? And why did they want Moose to repeat it at a press conference? There were many questions to be answered, and authorities were still unsure if they were hearing the garbled recording correctly. At 4:17 Monday afternoon, Moose once more stepped outside headquarters and spoke to the snipers through the press: "The person you called could not hear everything you said. The audio was unclear, and we want to get it right. Call us back so that we can clearly understand."[55]

Moose could not be sure if the snipers heard his message. But they had a message of their own for the authorities: one more killing in their deadly spree.

The Last Killing

At around 8:00 P.M. on Monday, October 21, a man walked into the Outback Steakhouse in Aspen Hill, Maryland, carrying a laptop computer. At some point during the evening he sat down in the check-in area of the restaurant, talking briefly to a customer but otherwise remaining alone. A surveillance camera captured the man on videotape. Later, he left the restaurant and drove away in an old, dark blue Chevrolet Caprice with tinted windows. John Allen Muhammad had returned to Aspen Hill, where he and Lee Boyd Malvo had killed cab driver Premkumar Walekar nearly three weeks before. He was there to kill again.

Early on Tuesday morning, thirty-five-year-old Conrad Johnson, a driver for the Montgomery County Ride-On commuter bus line, was about to begin his workday. A big man at 6 feet 2 inches (1.8m) and 250 pounds (113.4kg), "CeeJay" Johnson was a friendly and popular driver who had been on the job for ten years. His bus was parked in a staging area where

Conrad Johnson was shot and killed on this bus, which he drove in Montgomery County, Maryland.

drivers could have some coffee and get ready for their day's run. A public basketball court was nearby, and just beyond it a wooded area lay blanketed by the early morning darkness. Unseen in those woods, a Bushmaster rifle was pointed toward Johnson's bus, the crosshairs of its sight searching for the next victim.

At 5:55 A.M. Johnson was standing in the open doorway of the bus when a loud shot echoed off the cement basketball court. Johnson collapsed into the aisle of the bus, struck in the abdomen by a .223 high-velocity slug. A transit trainee who was to ride along with Johnson that day called 911. Johnson, still alive, was airlifted from the scene to Suburban Hospital in Bethesda. There he was attended to by James Robey, the

Investigators found this note in the wooded area from which the snipers aimed their shot at Conrad Johnson.

surgeon whose trauma team had desperately tried to save two other sniper victims, Sonny Buchanan and Lori Ann Lewis-Rivera. For Conrad "CeeJay" Johnson, the outcome was the same: He died in the hospital before his wife could arrive and say her last good-bye.

Local and federal law enforcement officials began their now-familiar routine of searching the nearby wooded area for clues. Before long they found one. A second Ziploc bag, with a note inside, was discovered stuck on a tree. Like the previous letter from the snipers, this note had red stars attached to it. But this time, the note could be read through the Ziploc bag without police having to wait for it to be opened in the forensics lab. Montgomery County police lieutenant Philip Raum copied the note on a piece of paper before the bag was sent to the lab. The writer's angry tone was clearly evident: "Can you hear us now? Do not play these childish games with us. You know our demands. . . . You departed from what we told you to say, and you departed from the time. Your incompetence has cost you another life."[56] The note set a new deadline for depositing the $10 million into the credit card account, and it repeated the "duck in a noose" response to be made by authorities through the media.

Searchers found other clues in the woods: a black duffel bag with a pocketknife, a cotton swab, and other small items inside; and a single brown glove. Each was sent to be tested for fingerprints, DNA, and anything else that might link the clues to the snipers. Meanwhile, at the joint operations center several other leads that the task force had been tracking down were beginning to pay off.

Clues in Tacoma

It had been a week since Robert Holmes called the FBI tip line on October 17 and told the officer on duty that he might have some pertinent information about the snipers. Details of the call had been put into the FBI's Rapid Start database, where they had remained unexamined until Tuesday, October 22,

Becoming a Forensic Document Examiner

Job Description:
Forensic document examiners use high-tech investigative tools (microscopes, spectrum analyzers, X-rays, and other equipment) to determine the authenticity of documents; compare handwriting, hand printing, typewriter- and computer-generated text to known samples for matches; and often testify as expert witnesses in court.

Education:
A two-year apprenticeship with an experienced document examiner is the usual way to obtain the knowledge required for this job. A bachelor of science degree is recommended, however, and is required to work as a document examiner in the U.S. Secret Service, as well as to obtain professional certification.

Qualifications:
Forensic document examiners need excellent eyesight and a good knowledge of ink, papers, printing processes, typography, and the investigative process. The ability to objectively approach investigative work, a mind for details, and good communication skills are additional advantages.

Additional Information:
Certification as a forensic document examiner may be obtained through the American Board of Forensic Document Examiners.

Salary:
Varies widely, but a forensic document examiner working with the U.S. Secret Service can earn from $43,365 to $97,213.

when FBI agents in Tacoma finally interviewed Holmes. The ex-soldier related what he knew about his friend and army buddy, the man named John Allen Muhammad, and his so-called son, Lee Boyd Malvo. Holmes told the investigators that he thought Muhammad may have suffered a mental breakdown when his children were taken away. He said he feared for the safety of Muhammad's wife and children, who were now living somewhere in the Washington, DC, area. He gave the agents pieces of metal that Muhammad had used to try to make a silencer for the Bushmaster. And he mentioned the tree stump in his backyard that Muhammad had used for target practice.

Authorities now had more physical evidence a continent away from the shooting sites on the East Coast. On Wednesday, October 23, a team of FBI agents swooped down on Holmes's

FBI investigators search the backyard of Robert Holmes's house in Tacoma, Washington, where Muhammad and Malvo had stayed.

Tacoma property. The backyard was sectioned off with yellow police tape, and agents with metal detectors searched for bullet fragments and shell casings. The tree stump was sawed off close to the ground with a chain saw and then wrapped and sent to the FBI lab in Quantico for investigators to examine it for .223 caliber slugs.

Other evidence was turning up from the liquor store shooting in Montgomery, Alabama. Local crime lab technicians had found a fingerprint on the discarded gun catalog found at the Alabama crime scene, but it did not match any prints on file. The fingerprint was then sent to Washington, DC, where it was run through the FBI's Integrated Automated Fingerprint Identification System (IAFIS). This database, which keeps electronic fingerprint records and criminal histories for millions of subjects, quickly found a match. In December 2001 a woman from Jamaica and her teenage son had been detained by the INS in Bellingham, Washington, for being in the United States illegally. They were fingerprinted and released to await deportation. The woman was Una James, and the teenager was Lee Boyd Malvo. The report stored in IAFIS also mentioned Malvo's connection with John Allen Muhammad. Malvo's fingerprint was, in the words of an FBI agent, the "one piece of the puzzle"[57] that allowed authorities to begin solving the rest of the puzzle, and ultimately to reveal the identity of the DC Snipers.

The Snipers Exposed

The Sniper Task Force now had two names that could be linked to the DC Snipers. "We started running with it at that point," remarks a task force official. "We were excited that at that point, we had an identity to look for—something tangible for the first time."[58] Photos of Malvo taken by the INS were distributed to police departments around the country. Tracking down a lead that Muhammad had once lived in California, task force member William Sorukas, a U.S. marshal, called Ralph Garofalo, a marshal friend in San Diego, where the two had once worked together. Sorukas asked Garofalo to search motor vehicle

Searching for Prints

One of the most basic pieces of forensic evidence is the fingerprint. All people have them, and they are all different, which is why fingerprints are useful for identifying people, both innocent and guilty. The Integrated Automated Fingerprint Identification System (IAFIS) is a database of fingerprints maintained by the FBI's Criminal Justice Information Services Division. It is the largest biometric database in the world. Along with fingerprints, IAFIS also stores criminal history information that is submitted by state and local law enforcement agencies.

Using special remote software, local police departments can electronically search the IAFIS database for matches to fingerprints found at a crime scene. On average, it takes about two hours to receive a response from the system, a substantial reduction in processing time over the old manual system, in which a fingerprint search could take up to three months to complete. But criminals are not the only people who have fingerprints on file with IAFIS. Background checks for employment or licensing purposes often include the taking of fingerprints, which are then submitted to the FBI and stored in the IAFIS database.

records to see if he could find a driver's license photo for a John Allen Muhammad.

Sure enough, Garofalo soon found a small black-and-white picture of Muhammad. He called Sorukas back and asked how his friend wanted him to deliver the photo. Sorukas told him to e-mail it to him, adding, "Take a good look at the picture. You're getting one of the first views of one of the snipers in DC."[59] Still, Sorukas was not completely sure that John Muhammad of Tacoma was the same man implicated in the sniper shootings nearly 3,000 miles (4,800km) away.

Sorukas had contacted U.S. marshals in Baltimore to try to run down a lead that placed Muhammad in a recent

*By late October,
police knew
Muhammad's
license plate number
and were on the
lookout for his car.*

confrontation with a Baltimore police officer. Late on Wednesday evening, Sorukas got the details of the encounter, which were obtained through an exhaustive search of Baltimore Police Department radio tapes. On October 8, Officer James Snyder had noticed a man sleeping in a dark blue 1990 Chevrolet Caprice parked at a gas station. Snyder radioed in the license plate number—New Jersey NDA-21Z—but the search came up empty. Waking the man up, the officer checked his driver's license, which was a valid Washington State license. With no outstanding warrants to base an arrest on, Snyder let Muhammad drive off. But his radio calls, which included Muhammad's name and information about his car, were captured on tape at headquarters as a matter of routine.

Snyder had no idea he had been talking to one of the snipers. But two weeks later, when investigators tracked down the tape, the connection became clear in the mind of Sorukas: Muhammad, who had lived in Washington and had a license from that state, was also seen in the Baltimore area during the sniper spree. This, he knew, was their man.

At task force headquarters in Rockville, an announcement over the PA system broke through the din of the busy room: "We have a license plate and the car they're driving."[60] Shortly after 9:00 P.M., a BOLO was issued nationwide for John Allen Muhammad and Lee Boyd Malvo; the notice included a description and license number of the Caprice. By 11:00 cable news channels were broadcasting the names of the two sniper suspects and the description of the car. Finally, the people of the Washington, DC, area could put names and faces to the duo that had been terrorizing the area for three weeks. Now, all law enforcement had to do was find them.

At 11:50 P.M. Moose held another press briefing, advising the media that an arrest warrant had been issued for John Allen Muhammad. Muhammad was armed and dangerous, Moose warned. Then, trying once more to make contact, Moose spoke to the snipers: "You have indicated that you want us to do and say certain things. You asked us to say, 'We have caught the sniper like a duck in a noose.' We understand that hearing us say this is important to you. However, we want you to know how difficult it has been to understand what you want because you have chosen to use only notes, indirect messages, and calls to other jurisdictions. . . . Our word is our bond. Let's talk directly. We have an answer for you about your option. We are waiting for you to contact us."[61] But once again, Muhammad and Malvo did not contact the authorities.

CHAPTER 6

Endgame

For three weeks Muhammad and Malvo had roamed the Washington, DC, area killing innocent people with impunity, all the while taunting police with telephone calls and letters. The task force had used the latest computers and communication systems to coordinate the complex task of tracking down the snipers. But a simple mention of the snipers' license plate number on a radio program brought their deadly killing spree to a close. Ironically, the end of the road for Muhammad and Malvo began when a white van pulled into a darkened parking lot near a Maryland freeway.

In his job as a supermarket refrigeration systems technician, Whitney Donahue drove a white Ford Econoline van. Lately when he pulled into a supermarket parking lot, people looked fearfully at his van, wondering if this was the notorious sniper's vehicle police were searching for. After finishing a late-night service call in Virginia, Donahue, a resident of Greencastle, Pennsylvania, was heading home on Interstate 70. While listening to the radio he heard a report describing the sniper's vehicle that police were looking for: a 1990 blue Chevrolet Caprice with New Jersey plate number NDA-21Z. The report also gave the names of two suspects wanted in the killing spree. Donahue wrote down the information in the unlikely event that he might run across the car.

At around 12:30 A.M. on October 24, 2002, he was still an hour or so away from home. He decided to take a break at a rest area near Frederick, Maryland, about 50 miles (80.5km) northwest of Washington, DC. As he pulled into the parking lot, he noticed two cars already there. One was a dark sedan that Donahue realized, upon taking another look, was a blue Caprice.

DC Sniper Shooting Locations

Maryland

OCTOBER 3
Silver Spring, MD

OCTOBER 22
Aspen Hill, MD

OCTOBER 2
Aspen Hill, MD

OCTOBER 3
White Flint, MD

OCTOBER 2
Wheaton, MD

OCTOBER 3
Aspen Hill, MD

OCTOBER 3
Kensington, MD

OCTOBER 7
Bowie, MD

DC

OCTOBER 9
Manassas, VA

OCTOBER 14
Falls Church, VA

OCTOBER 3
Washington, DC

Virginia

OCTOBER 4
Fredericksburg, VA

OCTOBER 11
Fredericksburg, VA

OCTOBER 19
Ashland, VA

Potomac R.

Shenandoah R.

Atlantic Ocean

0   10 Miles

He looked at the car's license plate, then down at the notes he had taken from the radio report: The plate numbers matched.

Finding a parking space, Donahue called 911 on his cell phone, but he could not get a usable signal. He drove his van to another location in the lot and this time was able to connect with a police dispatcher. He said, "The 1990 blue Caprice that you-all are looking for is sitting at the rest area, Route 70 westbound on South Mountain. . . . I read the tag when I pulled in."[62] The officer on the line told him to wait there in his van, keeping the phone line open. Donahue did so for nearly three hours. A few minutes after Donahue's call to 911, a long-distance trucker named Ron Lantz pulled his rig into the rest area and

Charles Moose makes his way to a press conference to announce the arrest of the DC Snipers.

also spotted the Caprice. He, too, called 911 and was told to use his truck to block the rest stop entrance so the suspects could not leave.

Takedown

Maryland State Police lieutenant David Reichenbaugh was driving near the rest stop when he received a radio call from headquarters about the Caprice sighting. "Send every trooper you've got,"[63] Reichenbaugh replied. Soon Maryland state troopers swarmed around the perimeter of the rest area, sealing it off and closing down both directions of I-70. There was no way that Muhammad and Malvo could escape by car. If they tried to flee on foot through the dense woods that surrounded the rest area, police canine units were ready to spring into action. "If anyone comes running out of the woods," Reichenbaugh commanded, "let the dogs eat them."[64]

Next to appear on the scene was the SWAT team charged with capturing the suspects. Arriving in helicopters and patrol cars, nineteen members of the Maryland State Police, Montgomery County Police, and the FBI's Hostage Rescue Team assembled in the parking lot of a nearby McDonald's to plan the raid on the Caprice. Six men, led by FBI agent Charles Pierce, formed the assault team that would make the actual arrest. After consulting a diagram of the rest area drawn by one of the state troopers, the team practiced their technique on a squad car. The plan was to sneak up to the Caprice from the rear, then split into two groups of three men and approach each side of the car. They would smash the windows, open the doors, and remove the suspects from the car.

The still-unknown factor was what they would find inside the Caprice. No movement had been seen in the car, leading the officers to wonder if Muhammad and Malvo were even there. Perhaps they had abandoned the Caprice and were long gone. There was concern that the assault team could be walking into a trap, with the snipers waiting for them with guns at the ready.

Whatever awaited them in the darkness, the members of the assault team knew they had a job to do. At 3:15 A.M. someone called for radio silence. With traffic stopped on I-70, the usual din of vehicles zooming by on the interstate was absent. The only sounds were the low rumbling of the big rigs blocking the entrance to the rest area, and the engines of helicopters hovering nearby ready to assist if needed. At 3:19 the assault began.

Dressed in black and wearing helmets and ballistic vests with trauma plates, the members of the assault team crept silently through the woods toward the Caprice, their assault rifles at the ready. On Pierce's hand signal, the six men stormed the Caprice, shouting for the occupants to surrender. With swift precision, the team smashed the windows of the car and yanked open the doors, illuminating the interior with bright lights attached to their weapons. They found Malvo lying asleep on the front seat and pulled him out of the Caprice and onto the ground. Muhammad, who had been asleep in the rear seat, sat up and raised his hands as the agents dragged him through the open door and forced him to the pavement. The entire takedown, which went off without a hitch, took less than a minute. The snipers were handcuffed and turned over to Maryland State Police officers.

As they were led away to two waiting cruisers, Muhammad and Malvo looked more like impoverished drifters than brutal murderers. Their clothes were filthy, and they smelled as if it had been a long time since their last shower. "Man," one of the troopers said as the two were being led away, "if you would have gotten that ten million, I hope you would have at least bought a bar of soap."[65]

A Car Full of Evidence

John Allen Muhammad and Lee Boyd Malvo were now in custody, but they could not yet be charged with the sniper murders. Despite the tireless work of investigators over the preceding three weeks, there was still nothing to connect the pair with any of the recent killings. Muhammad's arrest was made

under a federal warrant for possessing a firearm while under an order of protection. Malvo was being held in custody as a material, or essential, witness to the liquor store shooting in Montgomery, Alabama. "We still did not have a complete case," recalls Moose. "It was still in my mind that no one had seen these suspects do anything. We needed to confirm all the existing evidence, and to find a weapon."[66] The case against Muhammad and Malvo as the DC Snipers hinged on finding conclusive evidence linking them to the crimes. With the scene at the rest area now secured, investigators were anxious to move in and gather that evidence.

At 8:30 A.M. the examination of the Caprice began. Conducting the search were David McGill, Montgomery County forensics investigator, and ATF ballistics expert Tim Curtis. One of the first things they noticed was that the rear seat of the car appeared to be askew. Taking a closer look, they discovered that the seat was hinged at the top so it could be pulled upward for access to the trunk from the interior of the car. Lifting up the seat, Curtis discovered the one piece of evidence everyone hoped would be there: the Bushmaster

Muhammad's car contained abundant evidence that could be used to convict him and Malvo.

XM15-E2S rifle. Handling the rifle carefully, Curtis removed it from behind the seat, noticing that the safety was off. He soon discovered that there was a live round in the chamber; the Bushmaster had been prepared to kill again.

There was much more to be found in the Caprice, but investigators wanted to make sure the evidence was correctly processed. If handled improperly, the evidence could become contaminated, making it useless to forensic investigators and destroying its value in a trial. Moving the Caprice with an ordinary tow truck surely would have disturbed vital clues in the car. Investigators located an enclosed trailer to transport the car to an indoor facility in Montgomery County.

Interview with the Snipers

While the Caprice was being towed away, Muhammad and Malvo were undergoing interrogation at Montgomery County police headquarters in Rockville. The two were placed in separate rooms upon arrival. Malvo was being questioned by detective Terry Ryan, while Muhammad was interrogated by detective Jim Drewry. Malvo refused to speak, answering Ryan's inquiries with hand and head gestures. To Ryan, Malvo was an arrogant young man who seemed to delight in playing games with the authorities. Malvo nodded in agreement when told that the investigation showed he and Muhammad were in the Montgomery County area on October 2 and 3, the first two days of the killing spree.

In another room, Drewry and FBI agent Jansen Jordan were interviewing Muhammad. Unlike Malvo, Muhammad answered Drewry's questions, talking about his military service, his marital difficulties, and his children. But when asked about the shootings, Muhammad refused to talk and instead requested a lawyer. With no further progress in the interrogations, late Thursday

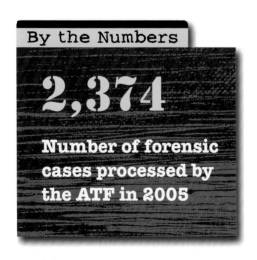

By the Numbers

2,374

Number of forensic cases processed by the ATF in 2005

A Boastful Killer

During his interrogation by police, Lee Boyd Malvo gradually became talkative, even bragging about the murders he and John Allen Muhammad had committed. Montgomery County detective June Boyle and FBI special agent Brad Garrett questioned the teenaged suspect at Montgomery County police headquarters. "Does it bother you to shoot people?" Garrett asked Malvo. "No," he replied. "Ninety-nine percent of the people couldn't do what I did. . . . What we did was unstoppable."

Of his fate, Malvo was indifferent. "Kill me, I don't care," he said. "Or torture me. Or if it takes bondage. Nothing bothers me. . . . You can't build a jail strong enough to hold me." Finally, Garrett asked if Malvo had any regrets. "I wouldn't change my life a bit," he said. "If I had it to do over, I'd do the exact same thing."

Quoted in Sari Horwitz and Michael E. Ruane, *Sniper: Inside the Hunt for the Killers Who Terrorized the Nation.* New York: Random House, 2003, p. 255.

afternoon the two suspects were taken to Baltimore for an initial court appearance before a federal judge. The judge declared that Malvo, who remained silent, be held for further investigation. In another courtroom Muhammad told the court, "I know where I'm at, and I know what I'm doing."[67] He was ordered to be held on the weapons charge.

The Killing Machine

After removing the Bushmaster from the Caprice, officers sent it to the ATF lab in Rockville for examination. Ballistics expert Walter Dandridge test-fired the rifle, and then compared the bullets to the fragments taken from the sniper victims. The markings on the slugs were a match in almost all the sniper shootings, conclusively proving that the Bushmaster was the murder weapon. Investigators also found fingerprints on the

During his testimony in Muhammad's trial, ATF agent Walter A. Dandridge Jr. holds the Bushmaster rifle used in the sniper shootings.

Bushmaster, and these were later matched to Malvo's prints which had been pulled from the gun magazine at the Alabama robbery scene. DNA samples on the rifle were also traced to both Muhammad and Malvo. The Caprice itself was called "a killing machine"[68] by a high-ranking law enforcement official. When ready to make a kill, the sniper could pull up the hinged back seat and crawl into the trunk, aiming the Bushmaster out of the hole cut into the trunk lid. The shooter never had to leave the car unless necessary for a better shot. When the Caprice was seized, investigators found a brown cotton glove shoved into the hole in the trunk. Tests confirmed that the glove was a match for the one found at the scene of the Conrad Johnson murder.

A thorough search of the Caprice turned up numerous items of physical evidence, many of which proved crucial in the case against Muhammad and Malvo. Investigators found a Sony Vaio laptop computer that had been stolen from a man named Paul LaRuffa during a robbery. LaRuffa was shot six times and left for dead, but he survived and later testified at Muhammad's trial. They also found a portable global positioning system (GPS) unit. The snipers had used the GPS along with a street mapping program in the laptop to plan their routes to and from shooting sites. Also recovered from the Caprice was an electronic organizer that contained incriminating evidence in the form of notes the snipers made to themselves on who deserved to die. Among those listed were a radio disc jockey, an operator at the FBI tip line, and journalists at Cable News Network (CNN). One remark stated, "Officer Derek is dead,"[69] referring to Derek Baliles of the Montgomery County Police.

A digital recorder found in the car contained a voice that, upon analysis, was determined to be that of Muhammad. The recording was the one played into the pay phone at the Exxon station near Richmond on October 21. ATF forensic chemist Edward Bender found trace evidence of nitroglycerin and primer residue in the trunk, indicating that a firearm had been discharged within the space.

For law enforcement authorities, especially those involved in analyzing the forensic evidence, hundreds of individual clues pointed to one inescapable conclusion: John Allen Muhammad and Lee Boyd Malvo were indeed the DC Snipers. Now it was up to a jury to look at that same evidence and determine whether the two men were guilty beyond a reasonable doubt.

Trial and Verdict

It was decided that the two would be tried separately in Virginia, where many of the sniper killings took place and where the death penalty could be imposed. On October 14, 2003, Muhammad's trial for the killing of Dean Harold Meyers began. At the outset, Muhammad acted as his own lawyer, saying, "I always felt I could speak better on my behalf."[70] But by

Muhammad as Lawyer

Several days into his trial, Muhammad petitioned Judge Leroy F. Millette Jr. to allow him to act as his own attorney. It was a highly unusual request from a man with no legal background who was on trial for his life. Nevertheless, Millette granted the request. On October 20, 2003, wearing a white shirt, dark tie, and sports jacket, Muhammad addressed the jury that would decide his fate.

Good evening. I would like to thank the judge for giving me the opportunity to speak. I want to talk to you briefly on some things that [the prosecutor] talked about. One of the things that we are here for today and the next couple days is to find out what everyone wants to know is what happened. Something happened. We have his side, and we have my side. . . . Something is wrong. Somebody is not telling the truth. Somebody's lying. . . . We are looking for evidence, and the evidence will show that . . . I had nothing to do with these crimes directly or indirectly, that I know anything about these crimes, that I know any times of these crimes or anything pertaining to these crimes at all.

Quoted in CNN.Com, "John Allen Muhammad's Opening Statement," October 20, 2003. www.cnn.com /2003/LAW/10/20/muhammad.statement/index.html.

the third day of testimony, Muhammad reconsidered his decision and allowed his lawyers to take over his defense.

During the trial, many forensic scientists took the witness stand to describe the evidence that had been found and how it linked Muhammad to the crime spree. Edward Bender discussed the chemical residue found in the Caprice's trunk. When Walter Dandridge took the stand, he displayed the Bushmaster XM15-E2S. Dandridge described for the jury how he compared bullet fragments recovered from the victims to

120 firearms and concluded that they were fired from the Bushmaster "to the exclusion of all other weapons."[71] David Coleman, an ATF fingerprint expert, testified that a fingerprint and palmprint found on the Bushmaster belonged to Malvo. John Hair, an expert from the FBI's Cyber Crime Squad, detailed the maps and other information found on the laptop computer, linking them to the sniper spree.

After five weeks of testimony, the case against John Allen Muhammad went to the twelve members of the jury. They deliberated for six hours before reaching a verdict: guilty of murder and conspiracy. Although Malvo had told investigators he had done the shooting, as the mastermind behind the spree,

Lee Boyd Malvo (center) is brought into court to be identified by a witness during Muhammad's trial.

Muhammad was as responsible as if he had pulled the trigger himself. On March 9, 2004, Muhammad was sentenced to death by lethal injection.

Lee Boyd Malvo went on trial on November 10, 2003, in Chesapeake, Virginia. Following his initial silence after he was arrested, Malvo became talkative with authorities, laughing as he bragged about the innocent people he shot. With these admissions confirming his guilt, his lawyers had to construct a defense that would somehow diminish Malvo's responsibility for his actions. They settled on an insanity defense as their strategy. They argued that Malvo had been brainwashed by Muhammad, who controlled the teenager so completely that he would do whatever Muhammad commanded, and kill

Family members of the sniper victims leave court after Muhammad was sentenced to death. Malvo was sentenced to life in prison.

whomever the elder man chose. Psychologists for both sides took the stand, setting forth differing opinions as to whether Malvo did or did not understand the difference between right and wrong during the sniper shooting spree. But the jury was not persuaded by the defense's efforts. After deliberating for two days, the jurors found Malvo guilty of the same crimes that Muhammad had been convicted of in his earlier trial.

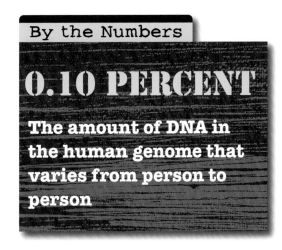

By the Numbers

0.10 PERCENT

The amount of DNA in the human genome that varies from person to person

After the verdict was reached, the jury retired to consider the sentence. Virginia is one of only a few states that have executed a juvenile for committing a capital crime at the age of sixteen or seventeen. But the young sniper avoided the sentence his accomplice received. Two days before Christmas in 2003, Lee Boyd Malvo was given the ultimate gift: His life was spared. He will spend the rest of his days in prison.

Aftermath

In the aftermath of the DC Sniper shootings of October 2002, many lives have changed. John Allen Muhammad remains on death row while attorneys pursue the automatic appeals that follow a death sentence. On April 22, 2005, the Virginia Supreme Court upheld the death penalty for Muhammad. Lee Boyd Malvo is captive within prison walls, knowing that he will never again walk free outside them. In May 2006 Muhammad went on trial in Rockville, this time for the murders of Conrad Johnson and the five other victims killed in Montgomery County. Although Muhammad had already received the death penalty in Virginia, the second trial was considered necessary in case the first conviction should some day be overturned on appeal. Mohammad was convicted of all six murders and on June 1 was sentenced to six consecutive life sentences.

Charles Moose resigned as chief of the Montgomery County Police Department to write a book about his experiences with the DC Sniper investigation. He received much criticism for trying to "cash in" on a tragedy that left ten people dead.

The families of the sniper victims have had their lives altered forever by the senseless and vicious killings. While nothing can bring back their loved ones, perhaps the capture and conviction of Muhammad and Malvo has brought a sense of closure to a tragic period in their lives.

Of course, the DC Snipers may not have been caught—and certainly would not have been convicted—if not for the painstaking work of the many forensic scientists who labored tirelessly on the case despite a large number of crime scenes, a scarcity of hard evidence, and mounting pressure from the public to solve the murders. From the tiniest marks left on a fragment of a bullet to the telltale patterns of a latent fingerprint and the certainty of DNA evidence, forensics will continue to play a vital role in law enforcement. As current capabilities advance and new technologies emerge, the day will come when criminals like the DC Snipers will be caught swiftly, before they can embark on a rampage that claims the lives of numerous innocent victims.

Notes

Introduction: Two Bullets

1. Quoted in Tamra El-Khoury, "Prayer Book Turns Aside Shooting-Spree Bullet," FoxNews.com, October 3, 2002. www.foxnews.com/story/0,2933, 64794,00.html.

2. Quoted in Sari Horwitz and Michael E. Ruane, *Sniper: Inside the Hunt for the Killers Who Terrorized the Nation.* New York: Random House, 2003, p. 5.

3. Quoted in Horwitz and Ruane, *Sniper*, p. 15.

Chapter 1: A Deadly October Day

4. Quoted in Horwitz and Ruane, *Sniper*, p. 71.

5. Quoted in Angie Cannon, *23 Days of Terror: The Compelling True Story of the Hunt and Capture of the Beltway Snipers.* New York: Pocket Books, 2003, p. 12.

6. Quoted in Horwitz and Ruane, *Sniper*, p. 75.

7. Quoted in Horwitz and Ruane, *Sniper*, p. 82.

8. Charles A. Moose and Charles Fleming, *Three Weeks in October: The Manhunt for the Serial Sniper.* New York: Dutton, 2003, p. 16.

9. Quoted in Horwitz and Ruane, *Sniper*, p. 85.

10. Moose and Fleming, *Three Weeks in October*, p. 24.

11. Quoted in Horwitz and Ruane, *Sniper*, pp. 88, 89.

12. Quoted in Cannon, *23 Days of Terror*, p. 26.

Chapter 2: Bullets and a Telltale Card

13. Bureau of Alcohol, Tobacco, Firearms and Explosives, "About ATF." www.atf.gov/about/mission.htm.

14. Quoted in Mike Ahlers, "Sniper Victim Prayed That 'God Wouldn't Let Me Die,'" CNN.com, October 29, 2003. www.cnn.com/2003/LAW/10/28/muhammad.trial/.

15. Quoted in Horwitz and Ruane, *Sniper*, p. 113.

16. Moose and Fleming, *Three Weeks in October*, p. 86.

17. Moose and Fleming, *Three Weeks in October*, p. 87.

18. Quoted in Cannon, *23 Days of Terror*, p. 118.

19. Moose and Fleming, *Three Weeks in October*, p. 132.

20. Moose and Fleming, *Three Weeks in October*, p. 134.

21. Moose and Fleming, *Three Weeks in October*, p. 138.

22. Moose and Fleming, *Three Weeks in October*, p. 138.

23. Quoted in Moose and Fleming, *Three Weeks in October*, p. 92.

24. Quoted in Cannon, *23 Days of Terror*, p. 86.

Chapter 3: Profile of a Killer

25. Quoted in Katherine Ramsland, "Criminal Profiling, Part 1: History and Method. The Mind Hunters," Court TV Crime Library. www.crimelibrary. com/criminal_mind/ profiling/history _method/6.html.

26. Quoted in Moose and Fleming, *Three Weeks in October*, p. 150.

27. Moose and Fleming, *Three Weeks in October*, p. 151.

28. Quoted in Stephen Kiehl, "Fingerprint on Stolen Map Said to Link Defendant, Sniper Scene," *Baltimore Sun*, October 22, 2003. www.baltimoresun.com/news/local /crime/bal-te.md.sniper22oct220015 56,1,5221060.story?coll=bal-local-utility.

29. Quoted in Kiehl, "Fingerprint on Stolen Map Said to Link Defendant, Sniper Scene."

30. Quoted in Cannon, *23 Days of Terror*, p. 35.

31. Quoted in Associated Press, "Witness: Malvo Tried to Escape 'Situation' While Traveling with Muhammad in Summer 2002," Court TV News. www.courttv. com/trials/sniper/120203_malvo_ap.html.

32. Quoted in Horwitz and Ruane, *Sniper*, p. 20.

33. Quoted in Horwitz and Ruane, *Sniper*, p. 38.

34. Quoted in Cannon, *23 Days of Terror*, p. 169.

35. Quoted in Cannon, *23 Days of Terror*, pp. 169–170.

Chapter 4: A Message from the Snipers

36. Quoted in Horwitz and Ruane, *Sniper*, p. 158.

37. Quoted in Horwitz and Ruane, *Sniper*, p. 169.

38. Quoted in Stephen Kiehl, "During Sniper Crisis, Two Calls Prompted Two Different Replies," *Baltimore Sun*, October 31, 2003. www.baltimoresun. com /news/local/crime/bal-te.md.dis patch 31oct31,1,1032704.story?coll=bal-local-utility.

39. Quoted in Kiehl, "During Sniper Crisis, Two Calls Prompted Two Different Replies."

40. Moose and Fleming, *Three Weeks in October*, p. 196.

41. Quoted in Horwitz and Ruane, *Sniper*, p. 176.

42. Quoted in Moose and Fleming, *Three Weeks in October*, p. 250.

43. Quoted in Horwitz and Ruane, *Sniper*, p. 179.

44. Quoted in Cannon, *23 Days of Terror*, p. 190.

45. Quoted in Cannon, *23 Days of Terror*, p. 194.

46. Quoted in Cannon, *23 Days of Terror*, p. 195.

47. Quoted in Cannon, *23 Days of Terror*, p. 196.

Chapter 5: Assembling the Puzzle

48. Quoted in Moose and Fleming, *Three Weeks in October*, p. 247.

49. Quoted in Moose and Fleming, *Three Weeks in October*, p. 254.

50. Quoted in Moose and Fleming, *Three Weeks in October*, p. 254.

51. Quoted in Moose and Fleming, *Three Weeks in October*, p. 257.

52. Quoted in Horwitz and Ruane, *Sniper*, p. 195.

53. Quoted in Horwitz and Ruane, *Sniper*, p. 191.

54. Quoted in Cannon, *23 Days of Terror*, p. 208.

55. Quoted in Cannon, *23 Days of Terror*, pp. 213–214.

56. Quoted in Horwitz and Ruane, *Sniper*, p. 203.

57. Quoted in Cannon, *23 Days of Terror*, p. 187.

58. Quoted in Simon Duffy, "Closing the Net: How They Cracked the Case." CNN.com, October 25, 2002. http://archives.cnn.com/2002/US/South/10/24/sniper.case.cracked/index.html.

59. Quoted in Horwitz and Ruane, *Sniper*, p. 210.

60. Quoted in Cannon, *23 Days of Terror*, p. 238.

61. Quoted in *The Washington Post*, "Speaking to the Sniper," October 25, 2002. www.washingtonpost.com/wp-srv/metro/daily/graphics/sniper/communicate_102502.html.

Chapter 6: Endgame

62. Quoted in Horwitz and Ruane, *Sniper*, p. 221.

63. Quoted in Cannon, *23 Days of Terror*, p. 245.

64. Quoted in Cannon, *23 Days of Terror*, p. 245.

65. Quoted in Cannon, *23 Days of Terror*, p. 247.

66. Moose and Fleming, *Three Weeks in October*, p. 290.

67. Quoted in Horwitz and Ruane, *Sniper*, p. 241.

68. Quoted in Kelli Arems and Jeanne Meserve, "Source: Caprice was 'Killing

Machine,'" CNN.com, October 24, 2002. http://archives.cnn.com/2002/US/ South/10/24/sniper.killing.machine.

69. Quoted in Kerry Sipe, "Journal: Muhammad Trial Journal," *Norfolk Virginian-Pilot*, November 5, 2003. http:// home.hamptonroads.com/guestbook/jou rnal.cfm?startrow=345&question=1&id

=53&sort=forward.

70. Quoted in Horwitz and Ruane, *Sniper*, p. 258.

71. Quoted in Court TV News, "Bullet Fragments from Shooting Scenes Match Rifle Found in Sniper Suspect's Car," November 6, 2003. www.courttv.com/ trials/sniper/110603_ap.html.

For More Information

Books

Andrea Campbell, *Forensic Science: Evidence, Clues, and Investigation*. Philadelphia: Chelsea House, 2000. A good introductory overview of the various types of evidence found at crime scenes.

Sari Horwitz and Michael E. Ruane, *Sniper: Inside the Hunt for the Killers Who Terrorized the Nation*. New York: Random House, 2003. A fascinating and detailed account of the DC Sniper case from the first killing through the capture of Muhammad and Malvo and the trials that found them guilty. Includes a section of black-and-white photographs.

Tina Kafka, *DNA on Trial*. Farmington Hills, MI: Lucent, 2005. This book describes how DNA evidence is gathered, analyzed, and used in court to convict the guilty and free the innocent. Includes a chapter on the use of animal DNA in protecting wildlife.

David Owen, *Police Lab: How Forensic Science Tracks Down and Convicts Criminals*. Toronto: Firefly, 2002. Illustrated with numerous color photographs, this book describes all types of forensic evidence, and how such evidence was used in several real-life cases.

Herma Silverstein, *Threads of Evidence: Using Forensic Science to Solve Crimes*. New York:

Twenty-First Century, 1996. This book focuses on actual case histories in which forensic evidence was used to convict the guilty suspect. Cases examined include the Oklahoma City bombing and the Unabomber case.

Paul B. Weston and Charles A. Lushbaugh, *Criminal Investigation: Basic Perspectives*. Upper Saddle River, NJ: Prentice Hall, 2003. With fifty years of combined law enforcement experience, the authors present a comprehensive text on criminal investigation, including updates on the latest forensic technology and case studies.

Web Sites

Bureau of Alcohol, Tobacco, Firearms and Explosives (www.atf.gov/). Learn what the ATF does and how, and what it takes to become an ATF agent. Includes a list of the ATF's Most Wanted criminals, statistics on arson and firearms, and a special link to a site that teaches teens how to surf the Web safely.

DC-Area Suburban Sniper Case, Court TV.com (www.courttv.com/trials/sniper/). Includes articles on pretrial events and the trials of Muhammad and Malvo. Has links to photographs of the crime scenes, key documents in the case, and reports on geographic profiling and serial killers in history.

FBI Youth Grades 6th–12th, Federal Bureau of Investigation (www.fbi.gov/kids/6th12th/6th12th.htm). Learn all about the FBI on this special page of its official Web site. Features a history of the FBI, videos on a day in the life of a special agent, a quiz, and interactive games.

How Crime Scene Investigation Works, HowStuffWorks.com (www.howstuffworks.com/csi.htm). How crime scene investigators collect and analyze evidence, and how real-life CSIs compare with their television counterparts.

Journal: Muhammad Trial Journal, *Norfolk Virginian-Pilot* (http://home.hampton roads.com/guestbook/journal.cfm?question=1&id=53&sort=forward). A detailed day-by-day journal of John Allen Muhammad's first trial, written by Kerry Sipe, online news coordinator for the *Norfolk Virginian-Pilot*. Includes fasci-

nating testimony from forensics experts, witnesses, law enforcement officers, and relatives of the sniper victims.

Sniper Attacks: A Trail of Terror, CNN.com (www.cnn.com/SPECIALS/2002/sniper/). A great site to get a comprehensive overview of the DC Sniper case. Includes sections titled "The Suspects," "Cracking the Case," "The Victims," and "Community Reaction." Also includes links to photos, videos, and interactive graphics.

Sniper Shootings Coverage, Washington Post.com (www.washingtonpost.com/wp-dyn/metro/specials/shootings/2002). More newspaper coverage of the DC Sniper shootings. This site has a link to "Sniper Shootings," a particularly good interactive map of the DC area that pinpoints the various crime scenes of the sniper spree, as well as links to photo galleries, close-up diagrams, and satellite images of some of the shooting sites.

Index

Picture Credits

About the Author

Craig E. Blohm has written numerous magazine articles on historical subjects for children for more than twenty years, and has authored many books for Lucent Books. He has written for social studies textbooks and conducted workshops in writing history for children. A native of Chicago, Blohm and his wife, Desiree, live in Tinley Park, Illinois, and have two sons, Eric and Jason.

AD	FF	MU
AV	GR	NC
BO	HI	SJ
CL	HO	CNL JAN 07
DS	LS	

Some materials may be renewable by phone or in person if there are
no reserves or fines due. www.lakeco.lib.in.us   LCP#0390